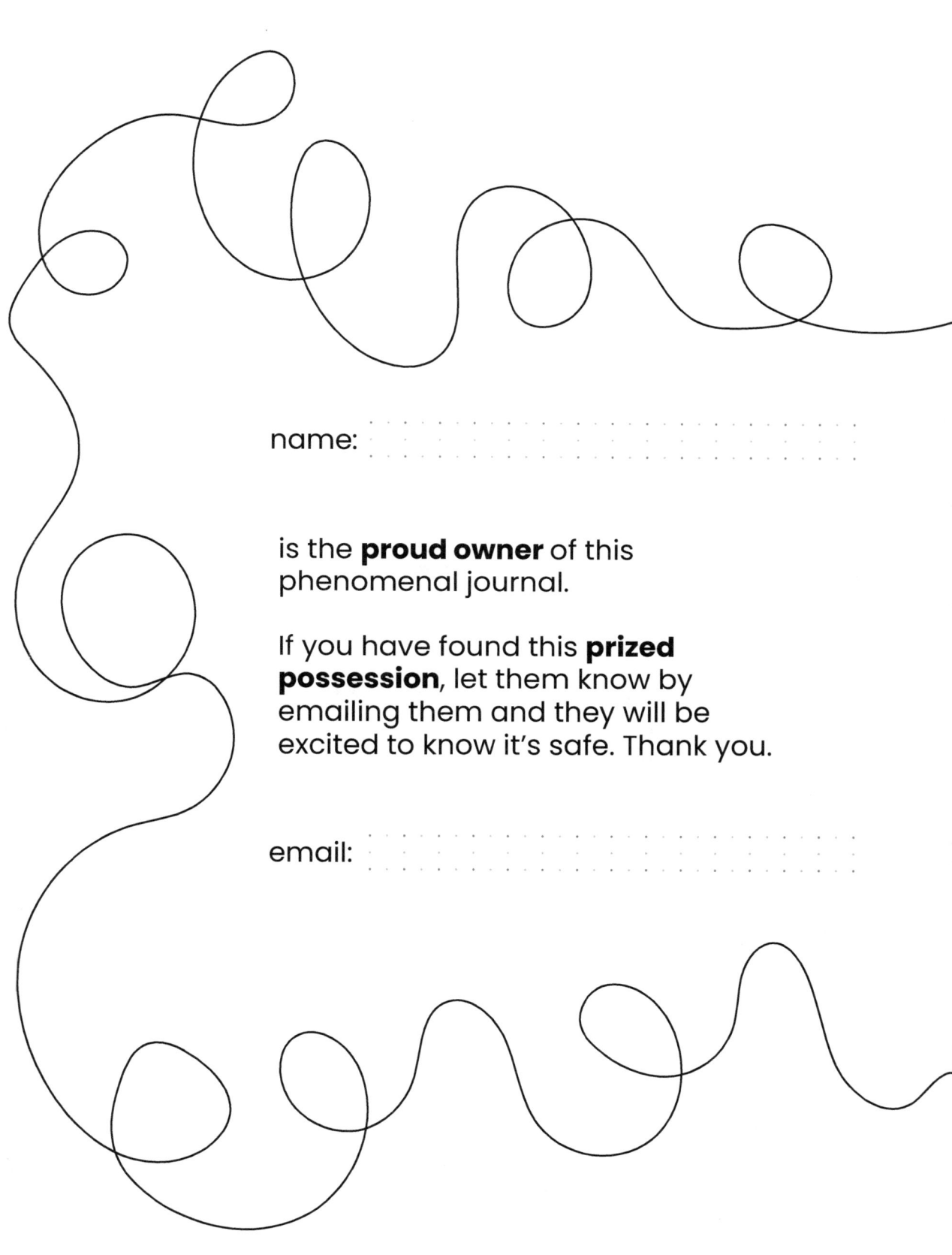

name: ....

is the **proud owner** of this phenomenal journal.

If you have found this **prized possession**, let them know by emailing them and they will be excited to know it's safe. Thank you.

email: ....

"Let go

Some **incredible things** are about to happen **for you.** Spend time each day with this journal — writing, reflecting, and getting creative.

As you do, you'll gradually **build confidence, happiness, and a healthier mindset** that will shine through in every aspect of your life.

What is the Shine Bright Journal?

It's a unique space designed to **help you cultivate Emotional Intelligence (EQ) and empathy.**

Curated by a Goleman Emotional Intelligence coach, Sandra Thompson, it's inspired by **psychology and neuroscience** to help you Shine Bright.

It builds in three steps:

 The tantalising truth about what makes us **incredible** human beings.

 Shining bright. Take some time to see how brightly you're shining **right now.**

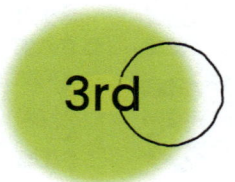 Pure brilliance. **Immerse yourself** here each day. Let your brightness shine through.

Samples from 1st & 2nd steps

Explore how humans experience life, and discover the incredible qualities that make you who you are. Dive into these exercises when it feels right for you.

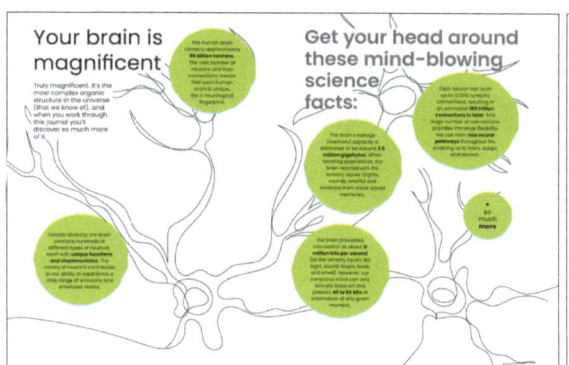

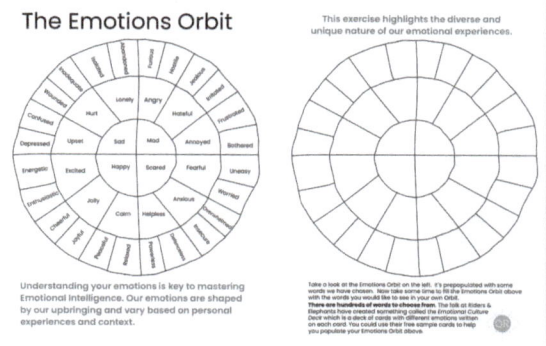

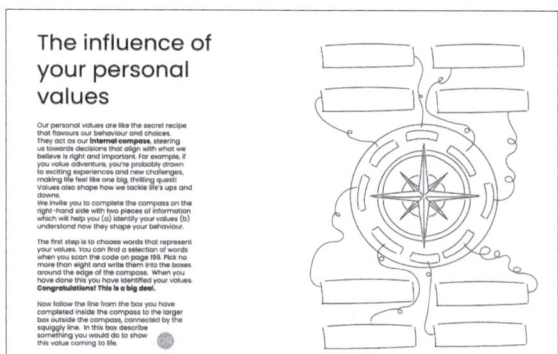

Samples from the 3rd step

Invest a few minutes each day in setting intentions and reflecting on your experiences. The daily ritual is incredibly good for you. You'll shine brighter and thrive over time.

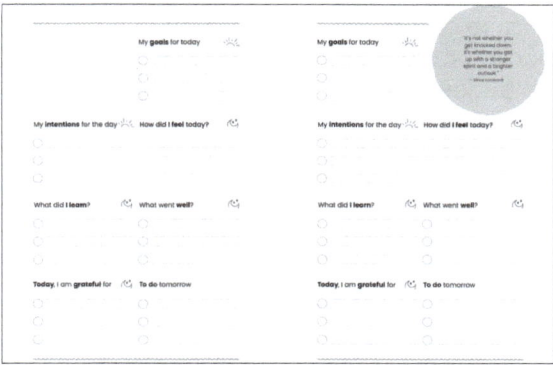

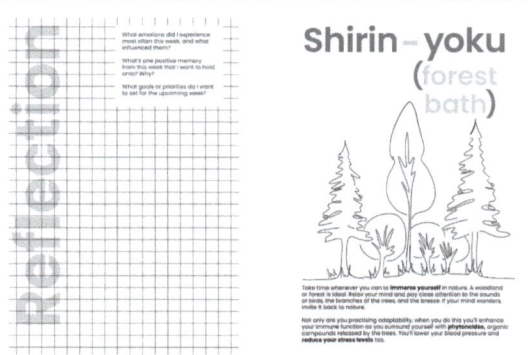

This space is uniquely yours, filled over time with your thoughts, dreams, wishes, and reflections. Here, you'll find reassurance, courage, support, and encouragement as you explore your inner world.

You already have everything within you to Shine Bright. This journal is here to help you uncover those inner treasures.

Supporting you along your journey:

We know that it can be daunting to work through exercises for the first time. We sometimes wonder "What am I expected to do here?"
To give you some confidence and reassurance, we have completed a few exercises as examples. We have also given you links to tools you can use to help you complete the exercises.

To find these examples and tools, look out for the QR symbol shown on the right. When you see this QR symbol go to page 199 and scan the relevant code.

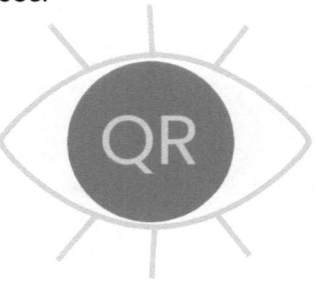

This Shine Bright Journal will help you have the brain space for brilliance

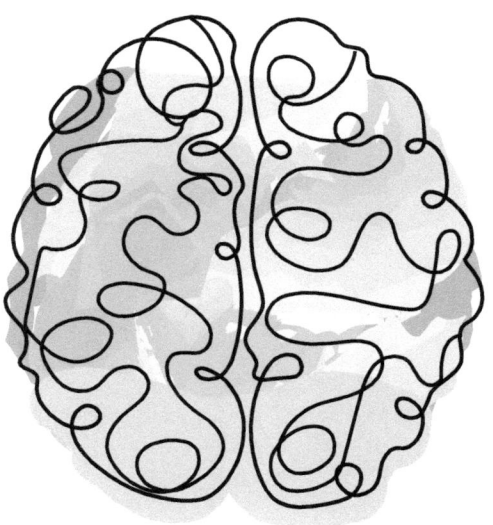 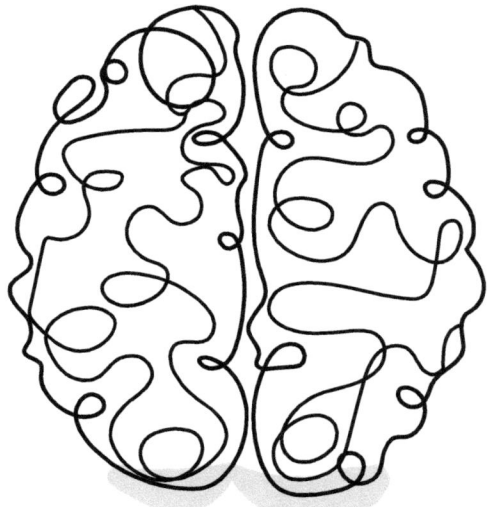

95%

When you try to remember, process, and juggle everything in your mind. **When you don't write things down,** you're keeping all of your thoughts, dreams, and wishes in the clutter with everything else.

15%

Mental **clarity** and greater **confidence.** When you keep a daily journal, you'll put the mental clutter onto the page and free up your brain for other things. This will help you to review, reflect, revive, rechange and rebound.

What makes us **incredible** human beings

Your brain is magnificent

Truly magnificent. It's the most complex organic structure in the universe (that we know of), and when you work through this journal you'll discover so much more of it.

The human brain contains approximately **86 billion neurons.** The vast number of neurons and their connections means that each human brain is unique, like a neurological fingerprint.

Cellular diversity: the brain contains hundreds of different types of neurons, each with **unique functions and characteristics**. The variety of neurons contributes to our ability to experience a wide range of emotions and emotional states.

Get your head around these mind-blowing science facts:

Each neuron can form up to 10,000 synaptic connections, resulting in an estimated **100 trillion connections in total**. This huge number of connections provides immense flexibility. We can form **new neural pathways** throughout life, enabling us to learn, adapt, and recover.

The brain's storage (memory) capacity is estimated to be around **2.5 million gigabytes**. When recalling experiences, the brain reconstructs the sensory inputs (sights, sounds, smells) and emotions from these stored memories.

+ so much **more**

The brain processes information at about **11 million bits per second** (all the sensory inputs like sight, sound, touch, taste, and smell). However, our conscious mind can only actively focus on and process **40 to 50 bits** of information at any given moment.

We're keeping three parts of the brain in mind for this journal...

Think of your brain as a quirky office.*

The **limbic system** is the drama queen, always feeling things intensely. The **prefrontal cortex** is the overworked manager trying to keep everyone in line. And the **parasympathetic** nervous system? That's the office zen master, always pushing for more yoga breaks.

Journalling is like giving your brain's manager a daily debriefing. It helps you **make sense** of the office drama, **spot patterns** in the chaos, and maybe **figure out** why Frank from Procurement always makes you want to hide in the cupboard, whether you're in the office or working from home! (Poor Frank, it's time for him to develop self-awareness.)

When you Shine Bright, you have greater emotional self-awareness — you can **recognise your emotions** and understand them; you'll be better at **managing your emotions** too! More about emotions on the next page.

* massive generalisations and oversimplification here, but you get the picture.

The Emotions Orbit

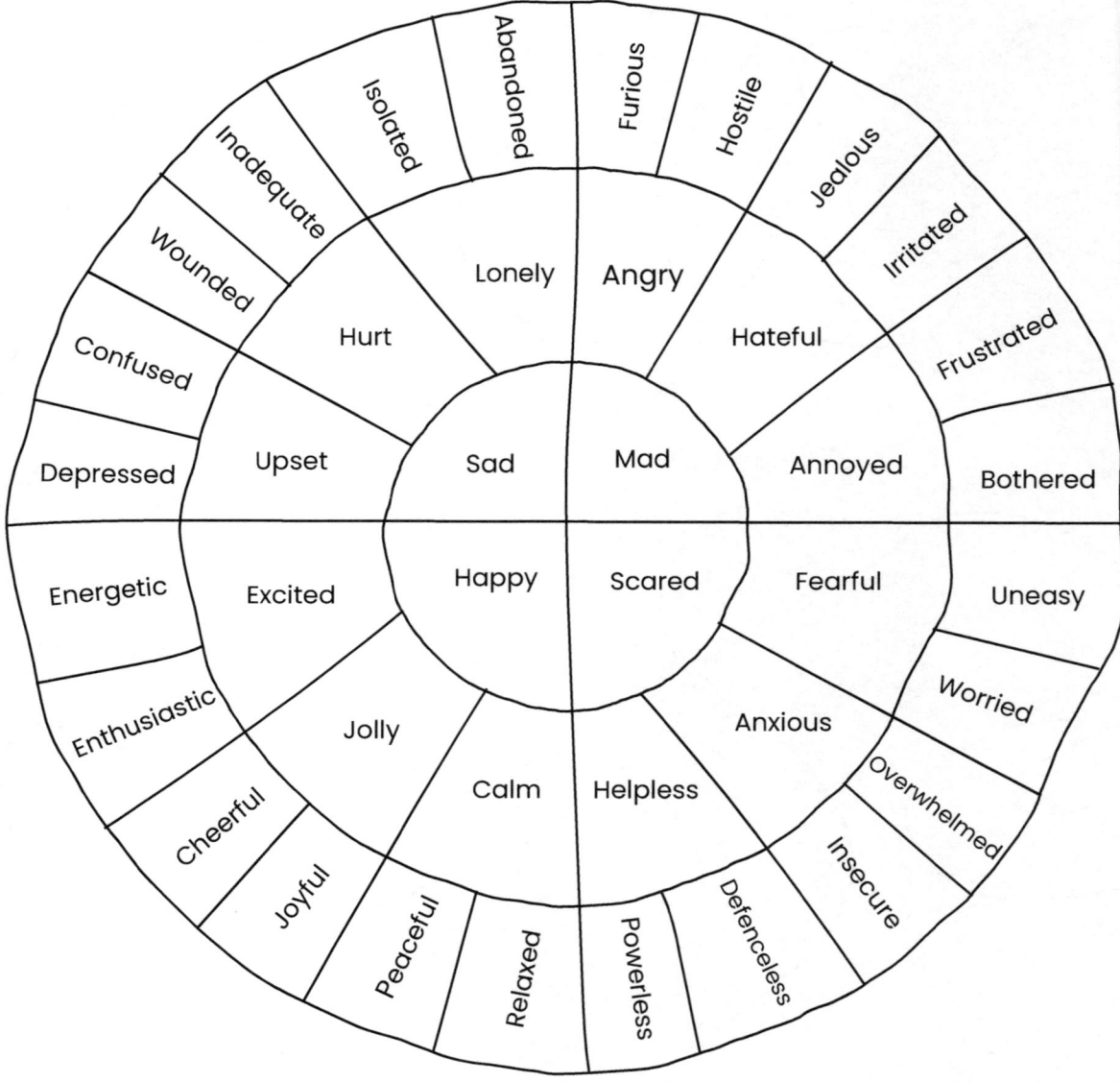

Understanding your emotions is key to mastering Emotional Intelligence. Our emotions are shaped by our upbringing and vary based on personal experiences and context.

This exercise highlights the diverse and unique nature of our emotional experiences.

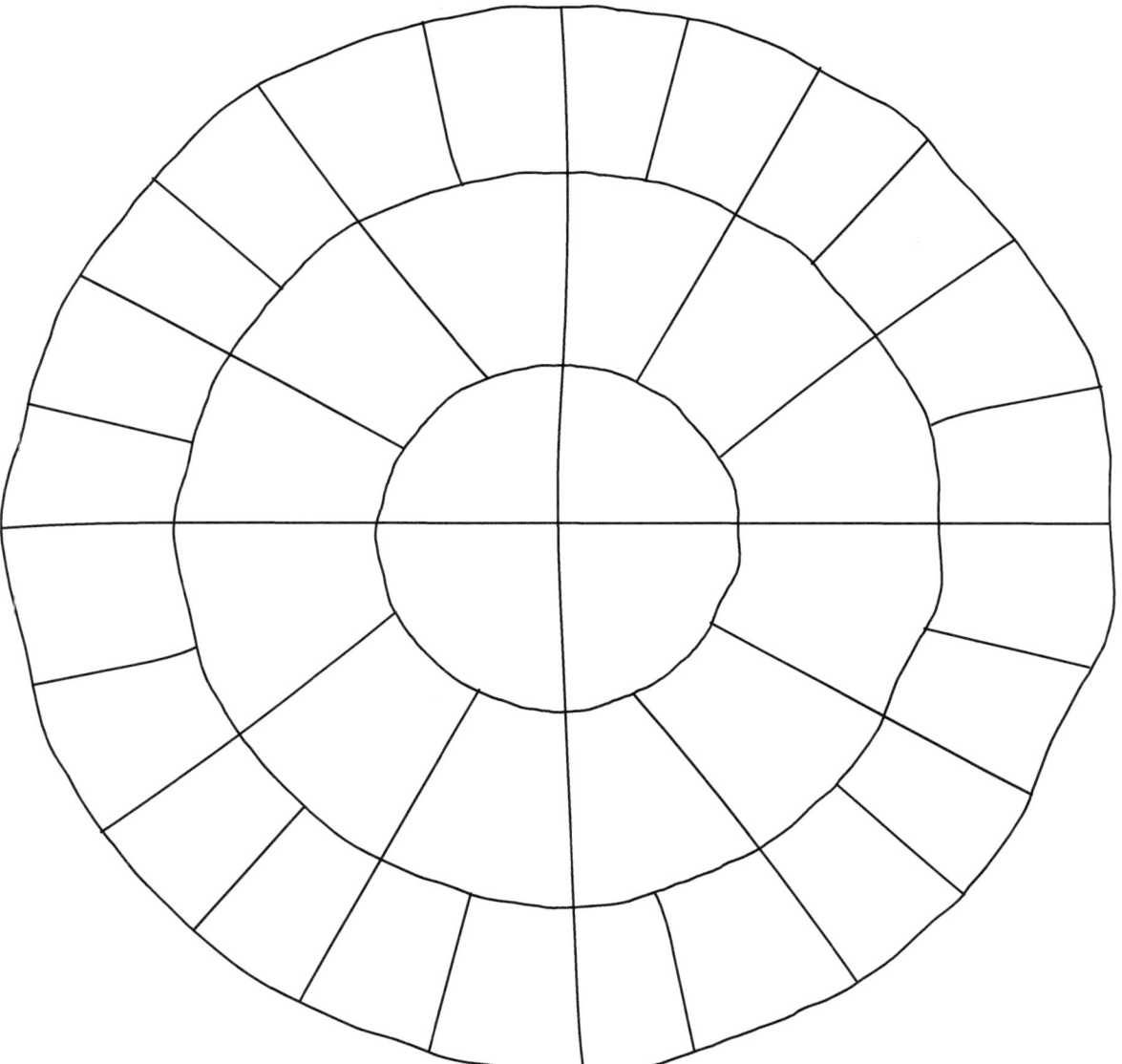

Take a look at the Emotions Orbit on the left. It's prepopulated with some words we have chosen. Now take some time to fill the Emotions Orbit above with the words you would like to see in your own Orbit.

There are hundreds of words to choose from. The folk at Riders & Elephants have created something called the *Emotional Culture Deck* which is a deck of cards with different emotions written on each card. You could use their free sample cards to help you populate your Emotions Orbit above.

You are an extraordinary human being, with a mind capable of remarkable achievements.

Your brain performs these feats not only because of all the amazing qualities we've outlined on page nine but also because it's a blend of logic, irrationality, complexity, and beauty. It operates intricate systems that allow you to navigate life. Like any powerful creation, however, it needs to be managed and maintained, as it can sometimes lead us astray, and certain thoughts it generates may limit our true potential.

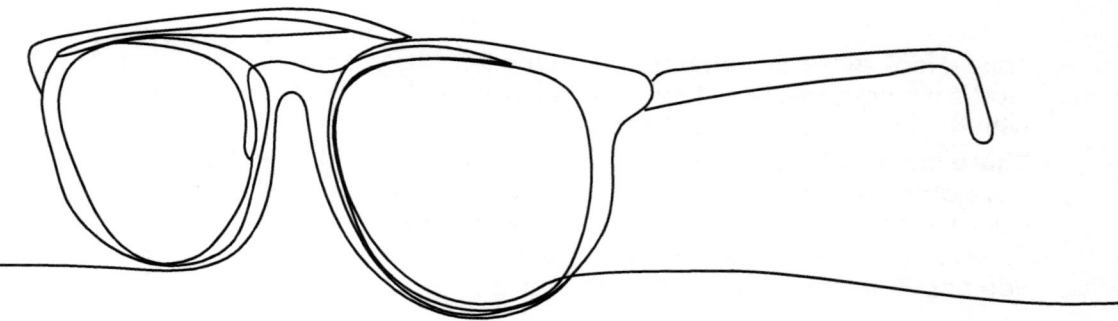

This brings us to biases — essential mental shortcuts that can be both incredibly useful and, at times, a real hindrance.

The late Daniel Kahneman had a great deal to say about biases. Here's a brief overview of what we need to understand about biases. The positive traits and the negative qualities, before diving into this journal.

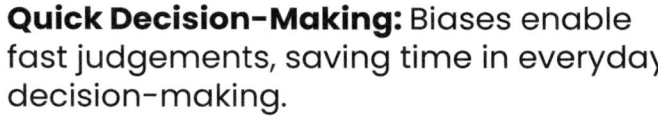

Quick Decision-Making: Biases enable fast judgements, saving time in everyday decision-making.
Pattern Recognition: They help us identify patterns and predict outcomes based on past experiences.
Emotional Resilience: Biases like optimism protect our mental well-being and keep us motivated.

Inaccurate Judgements: Biases can distort our thinking and lead to poor decisions.
Reinforcing Stereotypes: They can perpetuate harmful stereotypes and contribute to discrimination.
Limiting Growth: Biases restrict open-mindedness, limiting personal development and new opportunities.

Think of biases as sunglasses you are given as a child. They influence how you see the world. Your glasses might change as you grow up and experience different things. These experiences and the people you meet may influence your perception and change how you see the world. Depending on the type of bias, how aware you are of it and its usefulness to you, there's always the opportunity to change your lenses!

Realise the magic of Empathy & Emotional Intelligence.*

When you start to master the skill of Emotional Intelligence, you'll become much better at all of these things ...

- Understanding others' emotions.
- Managing your own feelings.
- Strengthening relationships.
- Resolving conflicts smoothly.
- Communicating with empathy.
- Reducing tension in stressful situations.
- Making wiser decisions.
- Building trust with others.
- Enhancing teamwork and collaboration.
- Adapting to different perspectives.
- Handling feedback constructively.
- Showing compassion in difficult times.
- Motivating and inspiring others.
- Recognising nonverbal cues.
- Responding calmly under pressure.
- Encouraging open dialogue.
- Navigating social dynamics gracefully.
- Supporting others through challenges.
- Balancing empathy with boundaries.
- Cultivating a positive work environment.

*This journal uses the Goleman & Boyatzis Emotional Intelligence 12 Competency model for reference.

"Emotional Intelligence is your ability to **recognise** and **understand** emotions in **yourself and others**. It's your **ability** to manage your behaviour and relationships."

(Goleman - Emotional Intelligence. Why it can matter more than IQ, 1995)

Companies that invest in Emotional Intelligence training see a 5-fold return on investment.

75% of careers are derailed due to emotional competence issues, including inability to handle interpersonal problems.

IQ contributes 20% to the success you experience in life. 80% of success depends on one's EQ.

Wowza

Plus much more ...

Explore the Shine Bright journal

This 12-week journal is an invitation for you to explore the 12 competencies of the Emotional Intelligence skill as described by
Goleman & Boyatis (HBR, 2017)

When you start each week of the 12-week journal you will recognise one of these four symbols on the right. There are exercises each week to introduce you to each competency within these four domains.

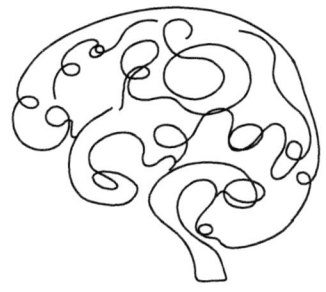

Emotional Self-Awareness

Emotional Self-Awareness

Emotional Self-Management

Emotional Balance
Adaptability
Achievement Orientation
Positive Outlook

Social Intelligence

Empathy
Organisational Awareness

Relationship Management

Influence
Coach and Mentor
Conflict Management
Teamwork
Inspirational Leadership

How **brightly** you already **shine**

I am.

This is incredible me ...

The probability of you existing as you, today, is approximately **1 in 10^2,685,000** - Dr. Ali Binazir.

**The probability is the same as having 2.5 million people each roll a trillion-sided dice, and all of them landing on the same number.
Wooooo hooooo, how incredible is that!**

We have left space here for you to fill with things that represent who you are. These might be **places, hobbies, people, tastes, favourites.** Whatever you want. Feel free to write, draw, stick, or colour as you wish.

Wow!

Just look at how far you've already come!

You were welcomed into the world

Take a moment to recognise and celebrate your achievements and challenges. Plot them on the timeline below. These experiences shape who you are. Enjoy this reflective exercise.

Today

Your personal Life Balance Tracker

Here you have three exercises in one. These Trackers have been designed so you can see which aspects of your life are going well and which aspects you might like to pay attention to. There are two Trackers (1) Now and (2) What you want your life to be like 18 months from now.

When you look at your life through the lens of the 10 themes around the edge of the Tracker, you get a **good picture of what you think your life is like.** Each aspect has 11 bars from the centre of the Tracker getting wider as they come out from the centre. Take a look at each aspect and give it a score based on how good you think your life is right now. Score from 1 to 11. (1 = poor and in urgent need of attention, and 11 = fantastic, wouldn't change a thing!) When you have decided the score for each of the aspects, fill in the spaces in pen or pencil from the centre outward. You might be delighted with work (10 out of 11) but know you don't spend as much time with your family as you would like (4 out of 11). Once you have filled in the Tracker on the right (Now) take a look. **What would you like to change?**

To complete the second part of this exercise, take a moment to decide **how you'd like your Life Balance Tracker to look** and then complete the one below.

The final part of the exercise is to decide what actions you want to take to get from the Tracker at the top to the Tracker beneath. Jot some ideas on these pages or make some notes at the back of this journal. Change takes time. **Be kind to yourself**.

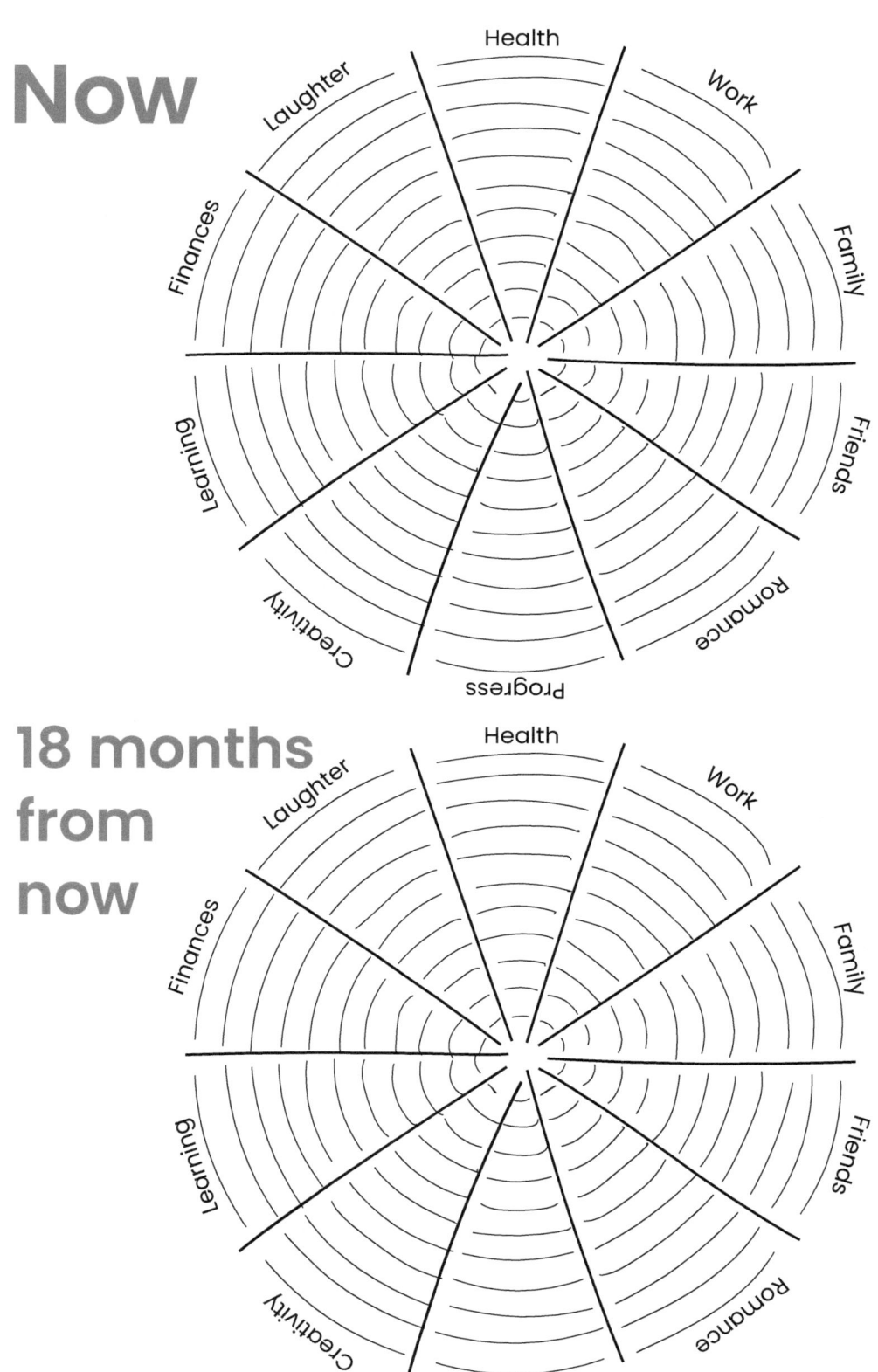

The influence of your personal values

Our personal values are like the secret recipe that flavours our behaviour and choices. They act as our **internal compass**, steering us towards decisions that align with what we believe is right and important. For example, if you value adventure, you're probably drawn to exciting experiences and new challenges, making life feel like one big, thrilling quest! Values also shape how we tackle life's ups and downs.
We invite you to complete the compass on the right-hand side with two pieces of information which will help you (a) identify your values (b) understand how they shape your behaviour.

The first step is to choose words that represent your values. You can find a selection of words when you scan the code on page 199. Pick no more than eight and write them into the boxes around the edge of the compass. When you have done this you have identified your values. **Congratulations! This is a big deal.**

Now follow the line from the box you have completed inside the compass to the larger box outside the compass, connected by the squiggly line. In this box describe something you would do to show this value coming to life.

18 months from now.

Welcome to your vision board exercise!

Gather magazines, newspapers, and other inspiring materials.
Cut out images, words, and symbols that represent the goals and dreams you want to achieve and make a reality 18 months from now. Arrange them and stick them down here.

Let your **brightness shine** through

Get ready...

There are a variety of things for you to do over the next 12 weeks. Each week will begin with an exercise; some weeks there will be two. Each exercise has been designed to get you to think about an Emotional Intelligence and empathy competency. Invest a few minutes each day in setting intentions and reflecting on your experiences. The daily ritual is incredibly good for you. You'll shine more brightly and thrive over time.

Weekday

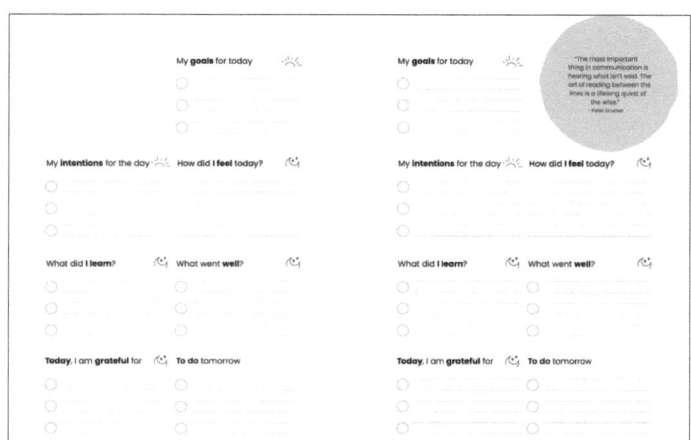

Reflection day + Exercise single page

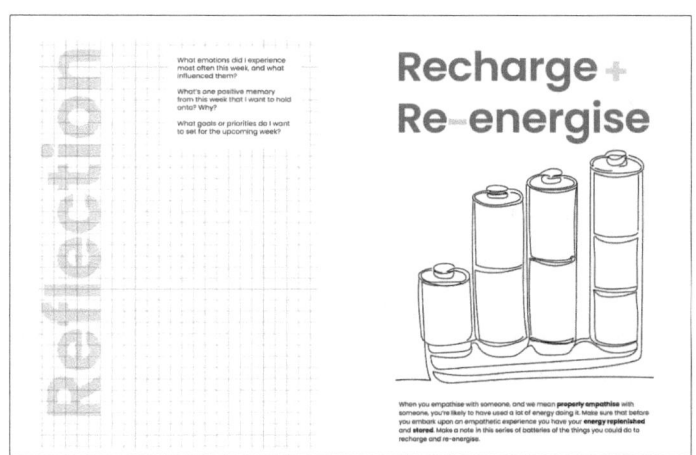

Exercise double page

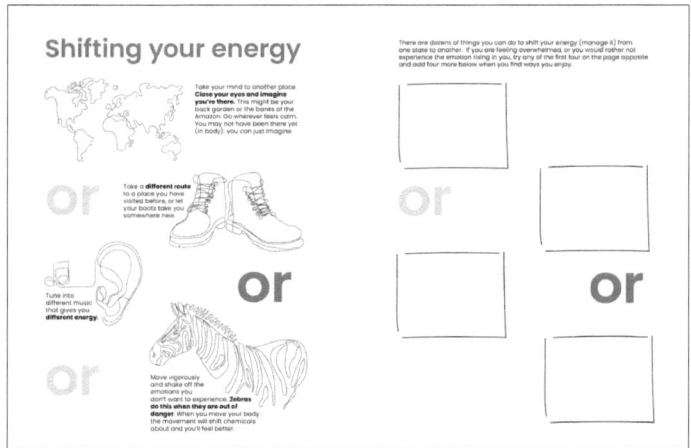

One we prepared earlier...

Embarking on a new journey can be daunting, especially when you're unsure where to begin. While this journal is your **personal canvas**, and you have complete **freedom to express yourself** as you see fit, sometimes a glimpse into others' approaches can spark inspiration.

We've included a few examples of completed journal pages as inspiration, not rules. You're the curator of this journey — follow, deviate, or forge your own path. What matters most is that it resonates with you. Your unique voice and experiences will make this journal valuable. Take a deep breath, trust your instincts, and let your thoughts flow freely...

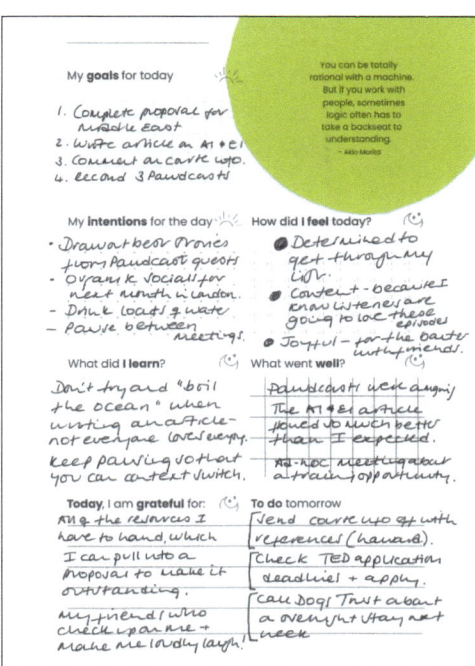
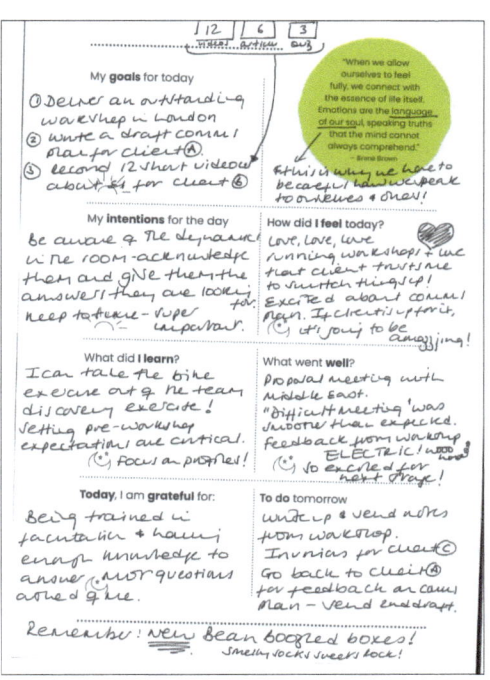
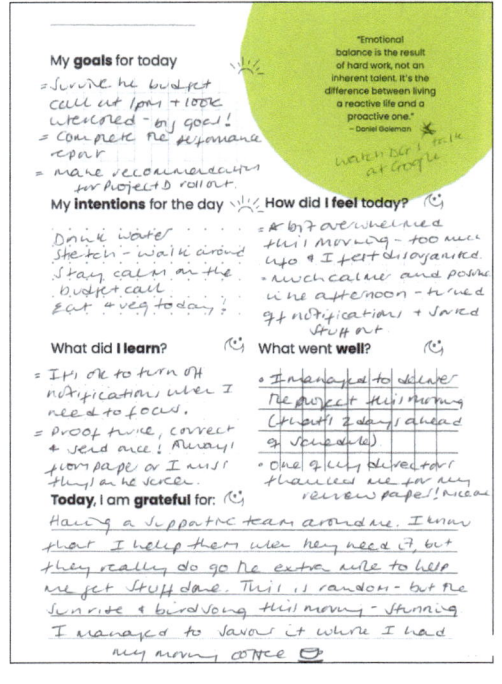
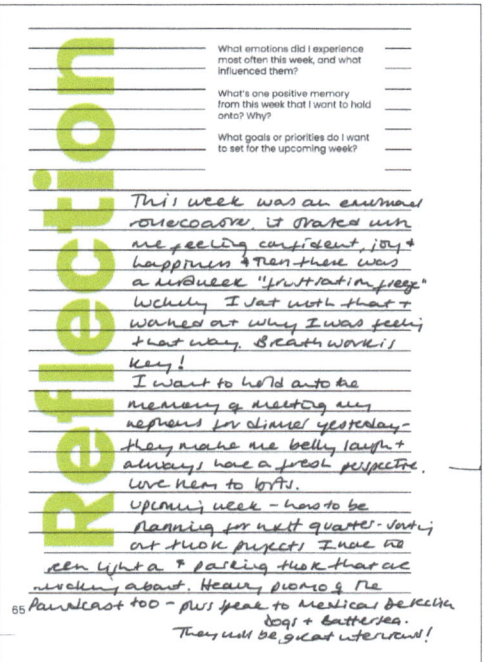

Let the adventure begin... with breath

Find a calm, quiet space and breathe:

1. **Inhale** slowly for 4 seconds.
2. **Hold** your breath for 4 seconds.
3. **Exhale** slowly for 4 seconds.
4. **Hold** your breath for 4 seconds.

Repeat this cycle for 2 minutes or longer.
As you see fit**...**

This technique helps regulate your breathing, activates the parasympathetic nervous system, and can reduce stress and anxiety. It's called "box" breathing because you can visualise each step as a side of a square.

Some of the emotions you experience may cause you to breathe rapidly and shallowly. You can influence your emotions when you manage your breathing.

The elevator of emotions

Some emotions lift us and some bring us down a bit.
Take a moment to think about the emotions you feel throughout the week.
Make a list of 10 beside the elevator above so that you can see the range of emotions you experience.
By listing 10 different emotions, you have started expressing **emotional granularity,** which means you're identifying different emotions and starting to describe them better. This is an important practice.

The emotion explorer

What happened?

Monday

Tuesday

Wednesday

Thursday

Friday

Saturday

Sunday

When you take the time to track the extreme or memorable emotions you experience over a week, you will **start to see patterns** and notable things that cause you to experience these emotions.

Take time at the end of each day in your first week to complete this, referring to the **most memorable emotion** you experienced that day.

You could use the Emotional Culture cards we mentioned when you were completing your Emotions Orbit (pages 13 — 14).

What emotions did you experience?	What thoughts did you have?

WEEK 1

My **goals** for today

- [ ] _____
- [ ] _____
- [ ] _____

My **intentions** for the day

- [ ] _____
- [ ] _____
- [ ] _____

How did **I feel** today?

_____
_____
_____

What did **I learn**?

- [ ] _____
- [ ] _____
- [ ] _____

What went **well**?

- [ ] _____
- [ ] _____
- [ ] _____

Today, I am **grateful** for

- [ ] _____
- [ ] _____
- [ ] _____

To do tomorrow

- [ ] _____
- [ ] _____
- [ ] _____

My goals for today

My intentions for the day

How did I feel today?

What did I learn?

What went well?

Today, I am **grateful** for

To do tomorrow

My **goals** for today

"When we allow ourselves to feel fully, we connect with the essence of life itself. Emotions are the language of our soul, speaking truths that the mind cannot always comprehend."
– Brené Brown

My **intentions** for the day

How did **I feel** today?

What did **I learn**?

What went **well**?

Today, I am **grateful** for

To do tomorrow

My **goals** for today

○ ....
○ ....
○ ....

My **intentions** for the day

○ ....
○ ....
○ ....

How did **I feel** today?

....
....
....

What did **I learn**?

○ ....
○ ....
○ ....

What went **well**?

○ ....
○ ....
○ ....

Today, I am **grateful** for

○ ....
○ ....
○ ....

To do tomorrow

○ ....
○ ....
○ ....

My **goals** for today

- ○ ....
- ○ ....
- ○ ....

> "There are no good or bad feelings, just information. Our emotions are our body's way of communicating with us. Listen to them without judgement."
> – Dr. Jill Bolte Taylor

My **intentions** for the day

- ○ ....
- ○ ....
- ○ ....

How did **I feel** today?

- ....
- ....
- ....

What did **I learn**?

- ○ ....
- ○ ....
- ○ ....

What went **well**?

- ○ ....
- ○ ....
- ○ ....

Today, I am **grateful** for

- ○ ....
- ○ ....
- ○ ....

To do tomorrow

- ○ ....
- ○ ....
- ○ ....

My goals for today

My intentions for the day

How did I feel today?

What did I learn?

What went well?

Today, I am **grateful** for

To do tomorrow

My goals for today

"Understanding your emotions is the first step to taking control of your life. When you own your feelings, they no longer own you."
- Anon

My intentions for the day

How did I feel today?

What did I learn?

What went well?

Today, I am **grateful** for

To do tomorrow

Reflection

What emotions did I experience most often this week, and what influenced them?

What's one positive memory from this week that I want to hold on to? Why?

What goals or priorities do I want to set for the upcoming week?

Stress Scheduler

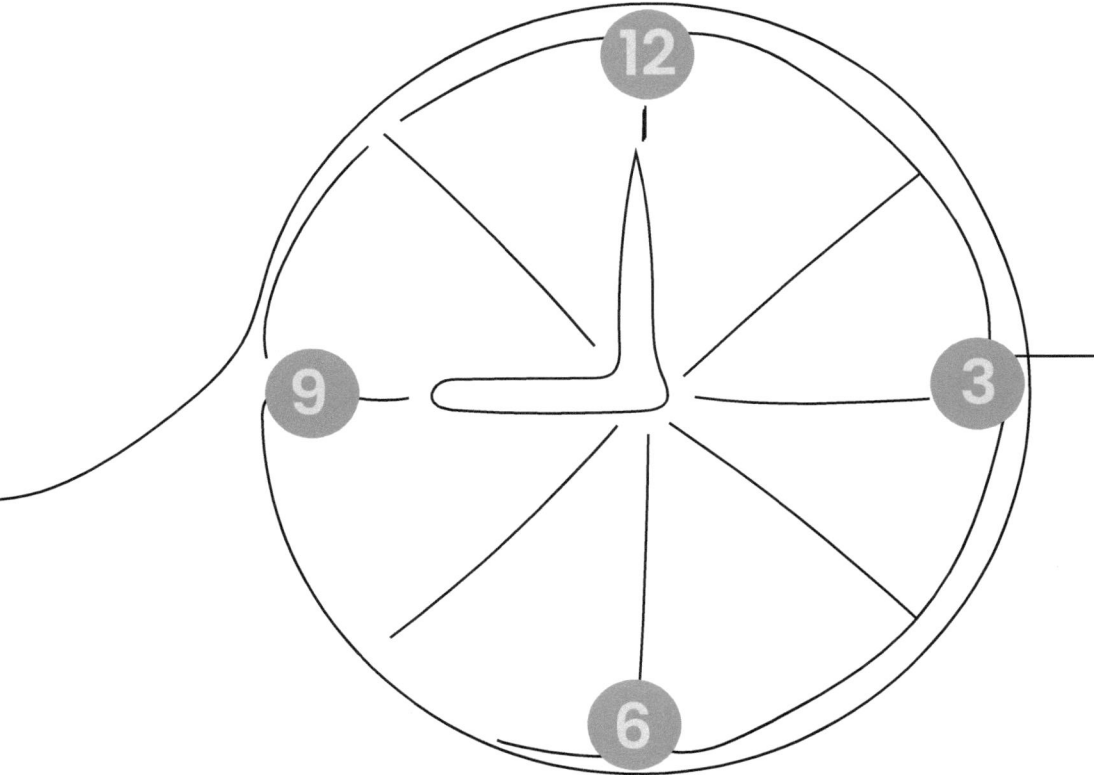

Emotions can overwhelm us, but we have many ways to manage them. One effective technique is the **Stress Scheduler**. Instead of letting stress disrupt your current moment, schedule a specific time to address it later. This allows you to acknowledge the stress without letting it derail your present focus. By **postponing** worry, you can stay productive and return to the issue when you're better prepared. When you next have a worry that is stopping your progress, come to this stress scheduler. What time is it? **What time, later that day would you prefer to worry about the thing that is stopping your progress?** Choose a time and write your worry into the closest segment to that time. Write it in pencil. Now close the book. You have written your worry down. You can always come back to the worry at the time you have scheduled. **Chances are that you will feel differently about the thing that was worrying you then.** This is just one way to manage your emotions.

Shifting your energy

Take your mind to another place. **Close your eyes and imagine you're there.** This might be your back garden or the banks of the Amazon. Go wherever feels calm. You may not have been there yet (in body); you can just imagine.

or

Take a **different route** to a place you have visited before, or let your boots take you somewhere new.

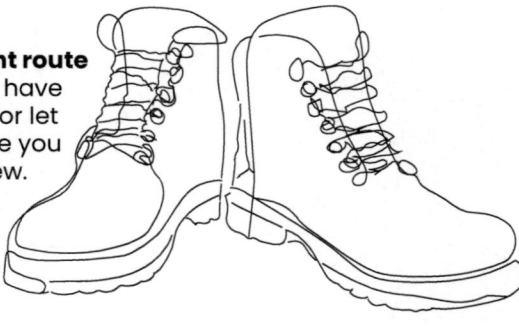

Tune into different music that gives you **different energy.**

or

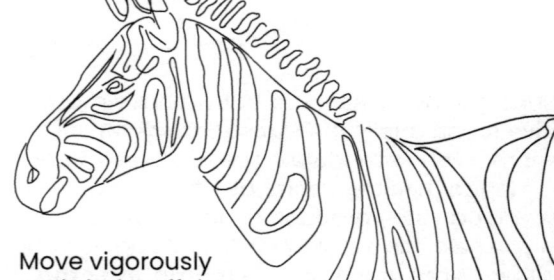

or

Move vigorously and shake off the emotions you don't want to experience. **Zebras do this when they are out of danger**. When you move your body the movement will shift chemicals about and you'll feel better.

There are dozens of things you can do to shift your energy (manage it) from one state to another. If you are feeling overwhelmed, or you would rather not experience the emotion rising in you, try any of the first four on the page opposite and add four more below when you find ways you enjoy.

or

or

or

WEEK 2

My **goals** for today

- [ ] _____
- [ ] _____
- [ ] _____

My **intentions** for the day

- [ ] _____
- [ ] _____
- [ ] _____

How did **I feel** today?

_____
_____
_____

What did **I learn**?

- [ ] _____
- [ ] _____
- [ ] _____

What went **well**?

- [ ] _____
- [ ] _____
- [ ] _____

Today, I am **grateful** for

- [ ] _____
- [ ] _____
- [ ] _____

To do tomorrow

- [ ] _____
- [ ] _____
- [ ] _____

My **goals** for today

My **intentions** for the day

How did **I feel** today?

What did **I learn**?

What went **well**?

Today, I am **grateful** for

To do tomorrow

My **goals** for today

> "You can't always control how you feel, but you can always choose how you respond. Mastering your emotions is the key to mastering your life."
> – Tony Robbins

My **intentions** for the day

How did **I feel** today?

What did **I learn**?

What went **well**?

Today, I am **grateful** for

To do tomorrow

My goals for today

○ ....
○ ....
○ ....

My **intentions** for the day

○ ....
○ ....
○ ....

How did **I feel** today?

○ ....
○ ....
○ ....

What did **I learn**?

○ ....
○ ....
○ ....

What went **well**?

○ ....
○ ....
○ ....

Today, I am **grateful** for

○ ....
○ ....
○ ....

To do tomorrow

○ ....
○ ....
○ ....

My **goals** for today

- ....
- ....
- ....

> "The ability to manage your emotions and remain calm under pressure has a direct link to your performance."
> – Travis Bradberry

My **intentions** for the day

- ....
- ....
- ....

How did **I feel** today?

....
....
....

What did **I learn**?

- ....
- ....
- ....

What went **well**?

- ....
- ....
- ....

Today, I am **grateful** for

- ....
- ....
- ....

To do tomorrow

- ....
- ....
- ....

My **goals** for today

My **intentions** for the day   How did **I feel** today?

What did **I learn**?   What went **well**?

Today, I am **grateful** for   **To do** tomorrow

My **goals** for today

_____

> "Emotional balance is the result of hard work, not an inherent talent. It's the difference between living a reactive life and a proactive one."
> – Daniel Goleman

My **intentions** for the day

How did **I feel** today?

What did **I learn**?

What went **well**?

Today, I am **grateful** for

To do tomorrow

Reflection

What emotions did I experience most often this week, and what influenced them?

What's one positive memory from this week that I want to hold onto? Why?

What goals or priorities do I want to set for the upcoming week?

Set a challenging goal & embrace an achievement mindset.

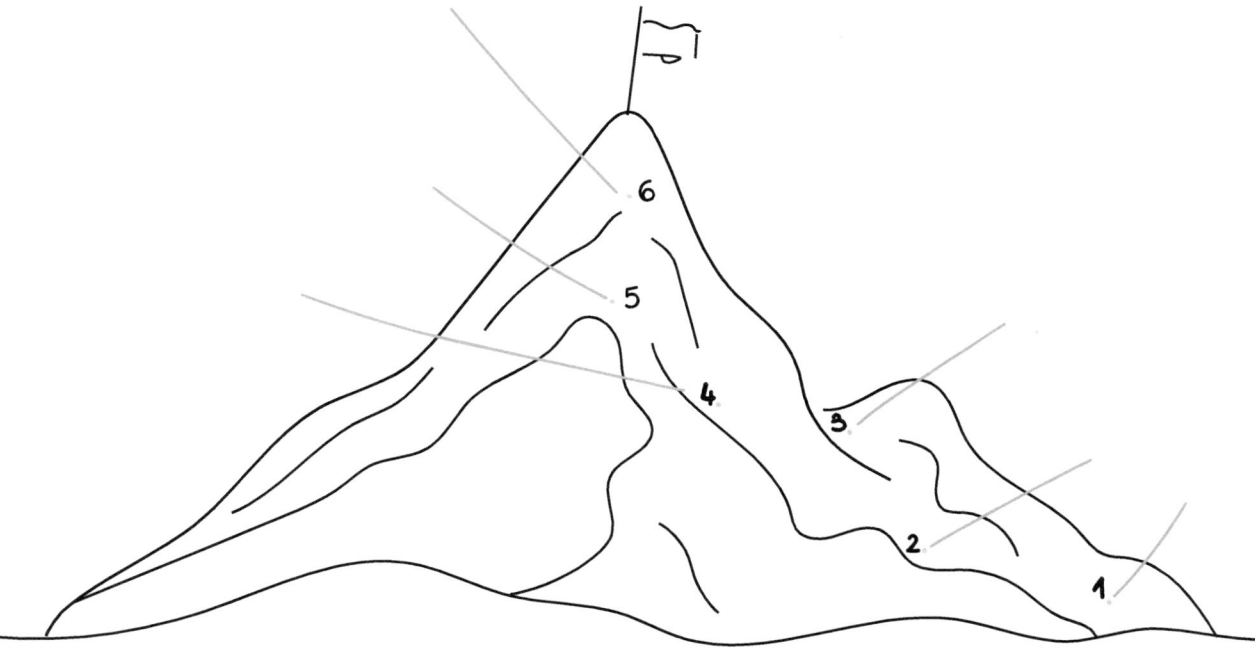

Take a look at the mountain above. Imagine that the flag at the top is your goal. Reaching a goal is easier when you know what **smaller steps** you need to take to get you there. To complete this exercise think of a goal you want to achieve. Consider the six smaller steps you need to take to get you there. Make a note of those six steps along the side of this mountain so you can see what you need to do (and you'll get to **appreciate the progress you make** as you approach the flag at the top!).

My **goals** for today

- [ ] _____
- [ ] _____
- [ ] _____

My **intentions** for the day

- [ ] _____
- [ ] _____
- [ ] _____

How did **I feel** today?

_____
_____
_____

What did **I learn**?

- [ ] _____
- [ ] _____
- [ ] _____

What went **well**?

- [ ] _____
- [ ] _____
- [ ] _____

Today, I am **grateful** for

- [ ] _____
- [ ] _____
- [ ] _____

To do tomorrow

- [ ] _____
- [ ] _____
- [ ] _____

"Achievement lies within the reach of those who reach beyond themselves."
– Bruce Lee

My goals for today

My intentions for the day

How did I feel today?

What did I learn?

What went well?

Today, I am **grateful** for

To do tomorrow

My **goals** for today

> "Dreams don't have to be big to matter; they just have to be yours. Pursue them with all your heart."
> – Sheryl Sandberg

My **intentions** for the day

How did **I feel** today?

What did **I learn**?

What went **well**?

Today, I am **grateful** for

To do tomorrow

My goals for today

○ ....
○ ....
○ ....

My intentions for the day

○ ....
○ ....
○ ....

How did I feel today?

○ ....
○ ....
○ ....

What did **I learn**?

○ ....
○ ....
○ ....

What went **well**?

○ ....
○ ....
○ ....

Today, I am **grateful** for

○ ....
○ ....
○ ....

To do tomorrow

○ ....
○ ....
○ ....

My **goals** for today

- ◯ ....
- ◯ ....
- ◯ ....

> "The future belongs to those who believe in the beauty of their dreams and work relentlessly to achieve them."
> – Eleanor Roosevelt

My **intentions** for the day

- ◯ ....
- ◯ ....
- ◯ ....

How did **I feel** today?

- ....
- ....
- ....

What did **I learn**?

- ◯ ....
- ◯ ....
- ◯ ....

What went **well**?

- ◯ ....
- ◯ ....
- ◯ ....

Today, I am **grateful** for

- ◯ ....
- ◯ ....
- ◯ ....

To do tomorrow

- ◯ ....
- ◯ ....
- ◯ ....

My goals for today

My intentions for the day

How did I feel today?

What did **I learn**?

What went **well**?

Today, I am **grateful** for

To do tomorrow

My **goals** for today

> "Success is the sum of small efforts, repeated day in and day out. An achievement-oriented mindset turns these efforts into milestones."
> – Robert Collier

My **intentions** for the day

How did **I feel** today?

What did **I learn**?

What went **well**?

Today, I am **grateful** for

To do tomorrow

Reflection

What emotions did I experience most often this week, and what influenced them?

What's one positive memory from this week that I want to hold onto? Why?

What goals or priorities do I want to set for the upcoming week?

Shirin - yoku (forest bath)

Take time whenever you can to **immerse yourself** in nature. A woodland or forest is ideal. Relax your mind and pay close attention to the sounds of birds, the branches of the trees, and the breeze. If your mind wonders, invite it back to nature.

Not only are you practising adaptability, when you do this you'll enhance your immune function as you surround yourself with **phytoncides,** organic compounds released by the trees. You'll lower your blood pressure and **reduce your stress levels** too.

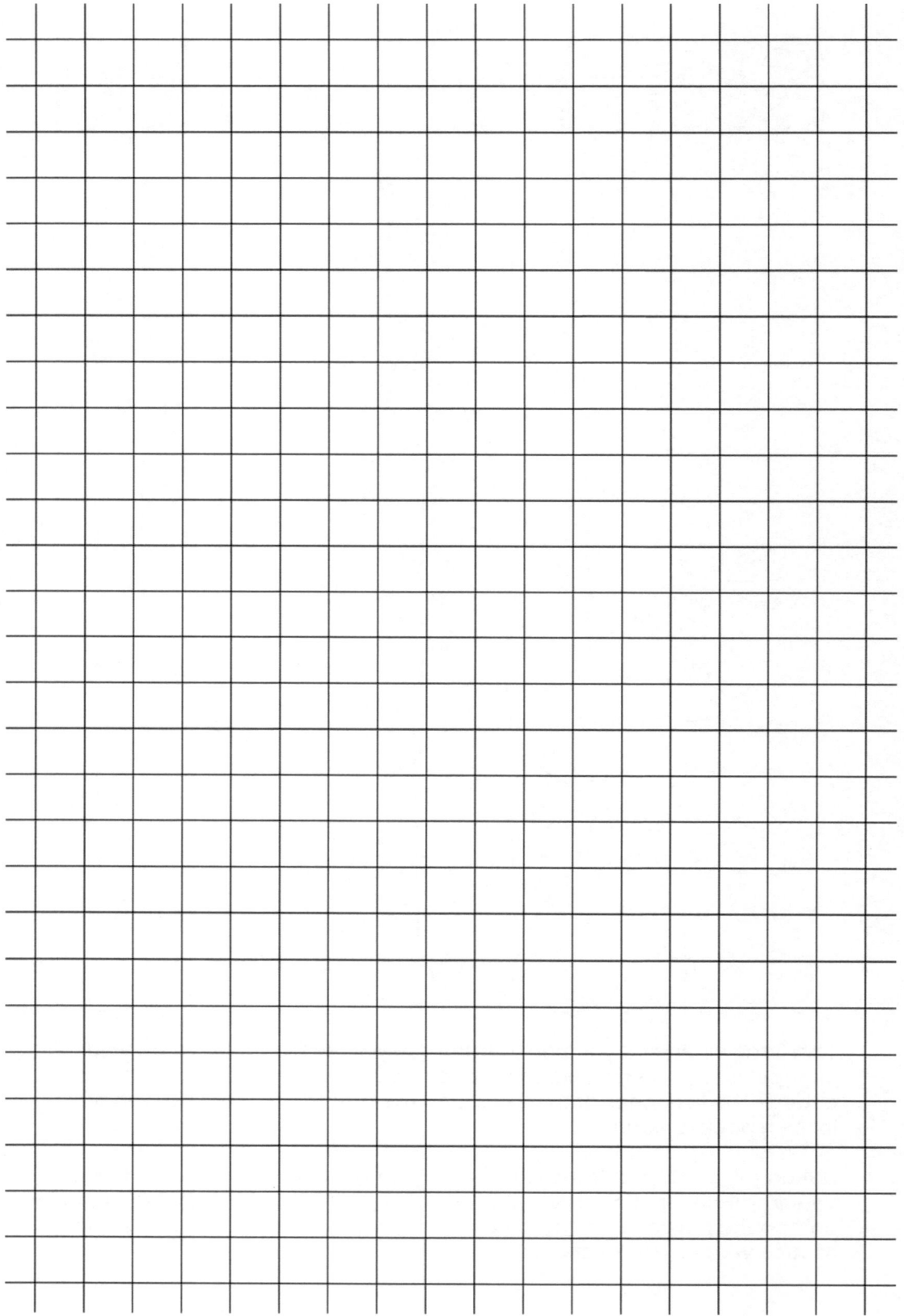

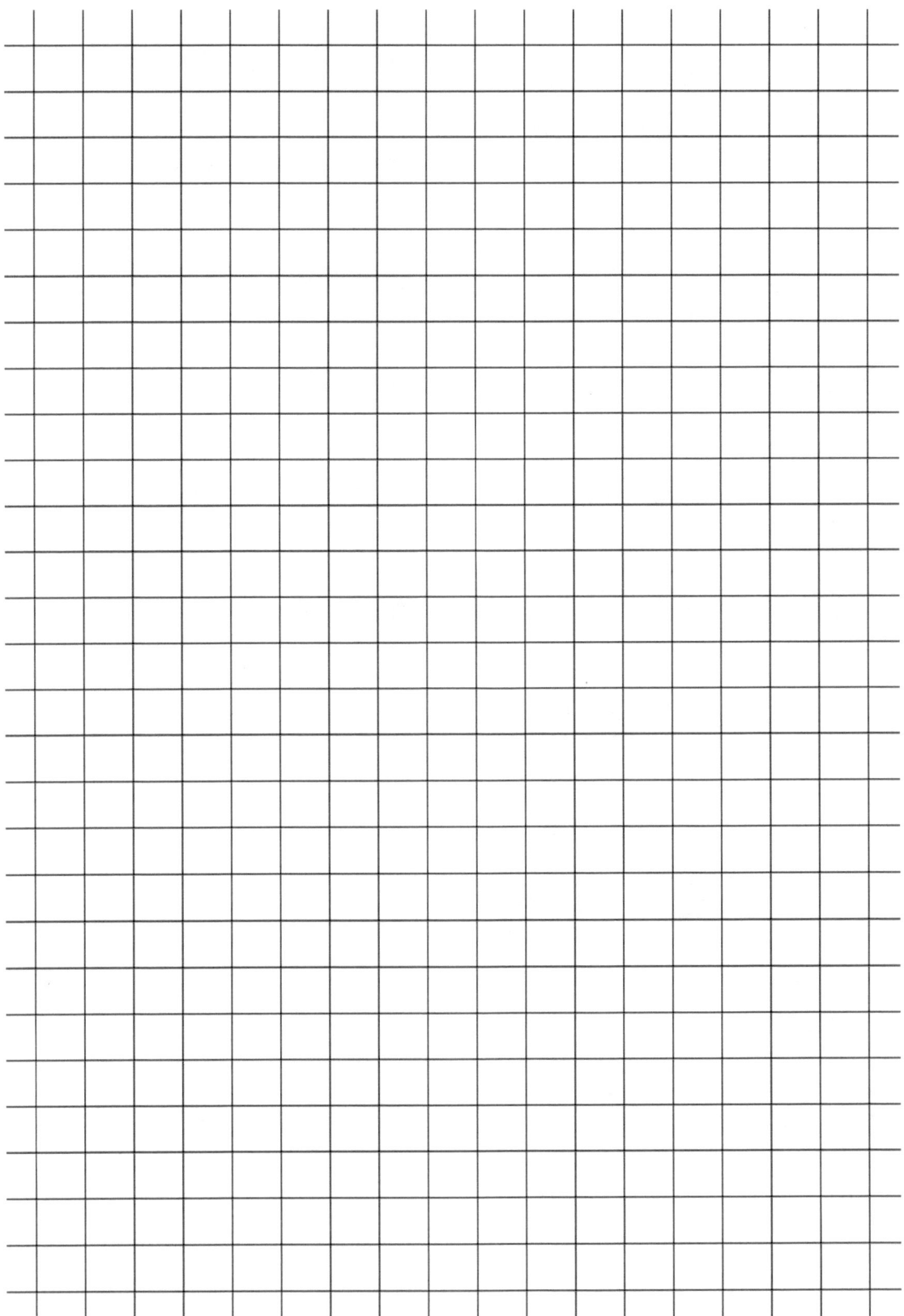

WEEK 4

My **goals** for today

- [ ] _____
- [ ] _____
- [ ] _____

My **intentions** for the day

- [ ] _____
- [ ] _____
- [ ] _____

How did **I feel** today?

_____
_____
_____

What did **I learn**?

- [ ] _____
- [ ] _____
- [ ] _____

What went **well**?

- [ ] _____
- [ ] _____
- [ ] _____

Today, I am **grateful** for

- [ ] _____
- [ ] _____
- [ ] _____

To do tomorrow

- [ ] _____
- [ ] _____
- [ ] _____

"The measure of intelligence is the ability to change."
— Albert Einstein

My goals for today

My intentions for the day

How did I feel today?

What did I learn?

What went well?

Today, I am **grateful** for

To do tomorrow

My **goals** for today

"When we are no longer able to change a situation, we are challenged to change ourselves. This adaptability is at the heart of emotional intelligence."
— Viktor Frankl

My **intentions** for the day

How did **I feel** today?

What did **I learn**?

What went **well**?

Today, I am **grateful** for

To do tomorrow

My goals for today

○ ....
○ ....
○ ....

My intentions for the day

○ ....
○ ....
○ ....

How did I feel today?

○ ....
○ ....
○ ....

What did **I learn**?

○ ....
○ ....
○ ....

What went **well**?

○ ....
○ ....
○ ....

Today, I am **grateful** for

○ ....
○ ....
○ ....

To do tomorrow

○ ....
○ ....
○ ....

My **goals** for today

- ....
- ....
- ....

> "The most difficult thing is the decision to act, the rest is merely tenacity."
> – Amelia Earhart

My **intentions** for the day

- ....
- ....
- ....

How did **I feel** today?

- ....
- ....
- ....

What did **I learn**?

- ....
- ....
- ....

What went **well**?

- ....
- ....
- ....

Today, I am **grateful** for

- ....
- ....
- ....

To do tomorrow

- ....
- ....
- ....

My goals for today

My intentions for the day

How did I feel today?

What did **I learn**?

What went **well**?

Today, I am **grateful** for

To do tomorrow

_____

My **goals** for today

"Adaptability is about the powerful difference between adapting to cope and adapting to win. It's a key trait of emotional intelligence."
— Max McKeown

My **intentions** for the day

How did **I feel** today?

What did **I learn**?

What went **well**?

Today, I am **grateful** for

To do tomorrow

Reflection

What emotions did I experience most often this week, and what influenced them?

What's one positive memory from this week that I want to hold onto? Why?

What goals or priorities do I want to set for the upcoming week?

Reframing your future

All sorts of people use this technique, especially very successful sports people. It's a technique called **visualisation**. All you have to do is think about something you need to do in the coming weeks and decide how you want that experience to be. You'll play it through a number of times in your head. **Every detail**, the place, the people, the smells, what you're wearing, what people say. Take a moment now to write the story of what happens in the stills below.

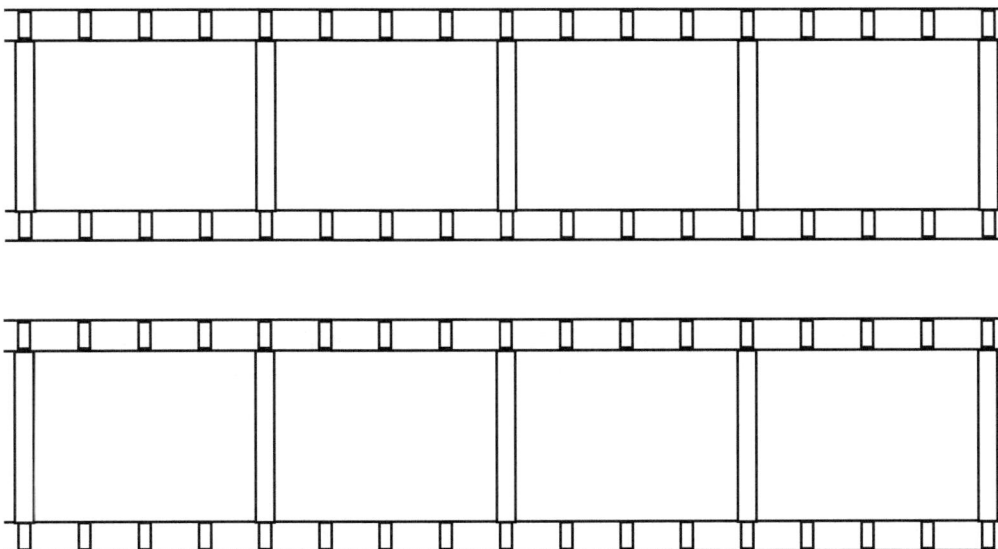

The brain does not distinguish between an event happening or being in your imagination, so if you pretend and visualise something you'll feel more confident (and you may even get the result you were expecting because you rehearsed it, like the athletes do) and in your brain you have done all of this before.

The weather with you

Imagine for a moment that your thoughts are like clouds. They are different shapes, they do different things. **Some protect us from the sun, make the sunset more beautiful, or they bring thunder or rain.**

We know that the clouds in the sky change all of the time. The wind blows them away or the shower comes and the clouds disappear.

Take a moment to write some of your thoughts, perhaps the less helpful thoughts, into the clouds on these pages. **In pencil.** Once you have filled your clouds in, decide if you want those thoughts or not. You might decide to shake like a zebra or go for a walk following a new path. Return to the clouds in this journal then and erase those thoughts that have dispersed from the page. **Remember that breath can help those thoughts move along too.**

WEEK 5

My **goals** for today

- [ ] _____
- [ ] _____
- [ ] _____

My **intentions** for the day

- [ ] _____
- [ ] _____
- [ ] _____

How did **I feel** today?

_____
_____
_____

What did **I learn**?

- [ ] _____
- [ ] _____
- [ ] _____

What went **well**?

- [ ] _____
- [ ] _____
- [ ] _____

Today, I am **grateful** for

- [ ] _____
- [ ] _____
- [ ] _____

To do tomorrow

- [ ] _____
- [ ] _____
- [ ] _____

"Believe you can and you're halfway there."
- Theodore Roosevelt

My **goals** for today

My **intentions** for the day

How did **I feel** today?

What did **I learn**?

What went **well**?

Today, I am **grateful** for

To do tomorrow

My **goals** for today

"You are braver than you believe, stronger than you seem, and smarter than you think."
– A.A. Milne

My **intentions** for the day

How did **I feel** today?

What did **I learn**?

What went **well**?

Today, I am **grateful** for

To do tomorrow

My goals for today

○ ....
○ ....
○ ....

My intentions for the day

○ ....
○ ....
○ ....

How did **I feel** today?

....
....
....

What did **I learn**?

○ ....
○ ....
○ ....

What went **well**?

○ ....
○ ....
○ ....

Today, I am **grateful** for

○ ....
○ ....
○ ....

To do tomorrow

○ ....
○ ....
○ ....

My **goals** for today

- ◯ ....
- ◯ ....
- ◯ ....

> "It's not whether you get knocked down; it's whether you get up with a stronger spirit and a brighter outlook."
> – Vince Lombardi

My **intentions** for the day

- ◯ ....
- ◯ ....
- ◯ ....

How did **I feel** today?

....
....
....

What did **I learn**?

- ◯ ....
- ◯ ....
- ◯ ....

What went **well**?

- ◯ ....
- ◯ ....
- ◯ ....

Today, I am **grateful** for

- ◯ ....
- ◯ ....
- ◯ ....

To do tomorrow

- ◯ ....
- ◯ ....
- ◯ ....

My goals for today

My intentions for the day

How did I feel today?

What did I learn?

What went well?

Today, I am **grateful** for

To do tomorrow

My **goals** for today

> "What's the worst that can happen? The person says no OR they might just say yes, and...! The possibilities are endless - you only need to ask."
> - Sandra Thompson

My **intentions** for the day

How did **I feel** today?

What did **I learn**?

What went **well**?

Today, I am **grateful** for

To do tomorrow

Reflection

What emotions did I experience most often this week, and what influenced them?

What's one positive memory from this week that I want to hold onto? Why?

What goals or priorities do I want to set for the upcoming week?

Recharge + Re-energise

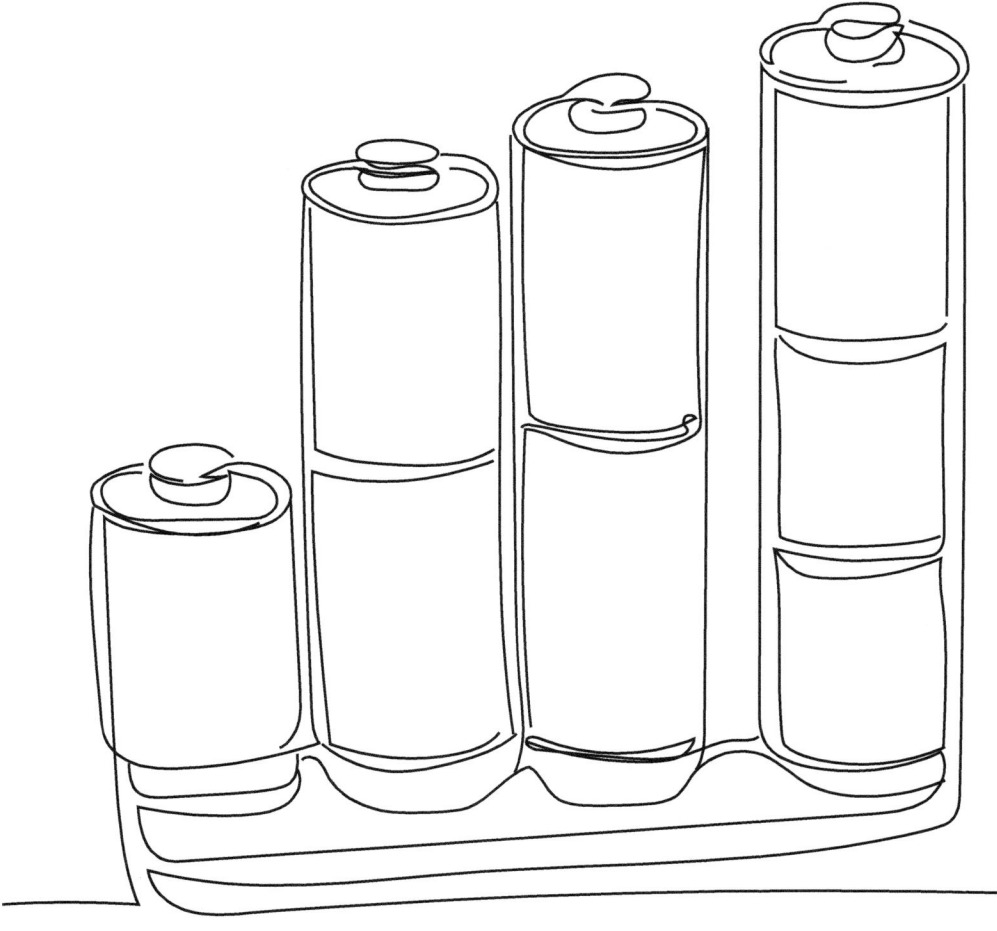

When you empathise with someone, and we mean **properly empathise** with someone, you're likely to have used a lot of energy doing it. Make sure that before you embark upon an empathetic experience you have your **energy replenished** and **stored**. Make a note in this series of batteries of the things you could do to recharge and re-energise.

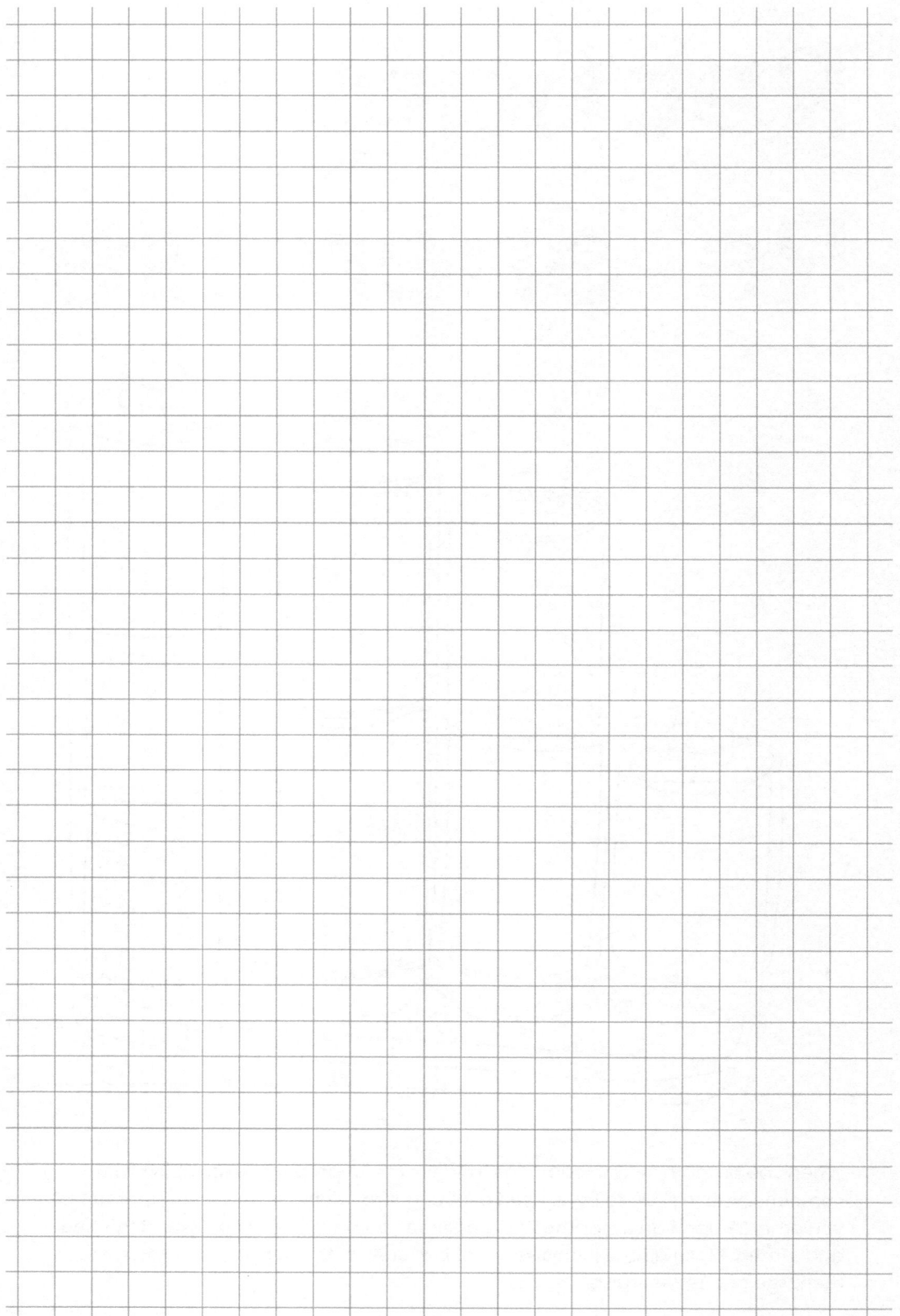

My **goals** for today

- [ ] _____
- [ ] _____
- [ ] _____

My **intentions** for the day

- [ ] _____
- [ ] _____
- [ ] _____

How did **I feel** today?

_____
_____
_____

What did **I learn**?

- [ ] _____
- [ ] _____
- [ ] _____

What went **well**?

- [ ] _____
- [ ] _____
- [ ] _____

Today, I am **grateful** for

- [ ] _____
- [ ] _____
- [ ] _____

To do tomorrow

- [ ] _____
- [ ] _____
- [ ] _____

"I think we all have empathy. We may not have enough courage to display it."
- Maya Angelou

My **goals** for today

My **intentions** for the day

How did **I feel** today?

What did **I learn**?

What went **well**?

Today, I am **grateful** for

To do tomorrow

My **goals** for today

> "Kindness in words creates confidence. Kindness in thinking creates profoundness. Kindness in giving creates love."
> – Lao Tzu

My **intentions** for the day

How did **I feel** today?

What did **I learn**?

What went **well**?

Today, I am **grateful** for

To do tomorrow

My **goals** for today

- ....
- ....
- ....

My **intentions** for the day

- ....
- ....
- ....

How did **I feel** today?

- ....
- ....
- ....

What did **I learn**?

- ....
- ....
- ....

What went **well**?

- ....
- ....
- ....

Today, I am **grateful** for

- ....
- ....
- ....

To do tomorrow

- ....
- ....
- ....

My **goals** for today

- ○ ....
- ○ ....
- ○ ....

> "Empathy has no script. There is no right way or wrong way to do it. It's simply listening, holding space, withholding judgment, emotionally connecting, and communicating that incredibly healing message of 'You're not alone'."
> – Brené Brown

My **intentions** for the day

- ○ ....
- ○ ....
- ○ ....

How did **I feel** today?

- ○ ....
- ○ ....
- ○ ....

What did **I learn**?

- ○ ....
- ○ ....
- ○ ....

What went **well**?

- ○ ....
- ○ ....
- ○ ....

Today, I am **grateful** for

- ○ ....
- ○ ....
- ○ ....

To do tomorrow

- ○ ....
- ○ ....
- ○ ....

My goals for today

My intentions for the day

How did I feel today?

What did I learn?

What went well?

Today, I am **grateful** for

To do tomorrow

My **goals** for today

> "Leadership is about empathy. It is about having the ability to relate to and connect with people for the purpose of inspiring and empowering their lives."
> – Oprah Winfrey

My **intentions** for the day

How did **I feel** today?

What did **I learn**?

What went **well**?

Today, I am **grateful** for

To do tomorrow

Reflection

What emotions did I experience most often this week, and what influenced them?

What's one positive memory from this week that I want to hold onto? Why?

What goals or priorities do I want to set for the upcoming week?

Where's the energy in the room?

Organisational awareness involves **reading the room** — understanding group dynamics and responding appropriately. Practise this by observing your next meeting of five or more people: note who **dominates**, who has attention **despite saying little**, who is **interrupted**, and who others listen to. List the five key observations in the shapes below.
When you practice **reading the room** you become better able to **influence** the people in the room because you understand the **power dynamics** much better.

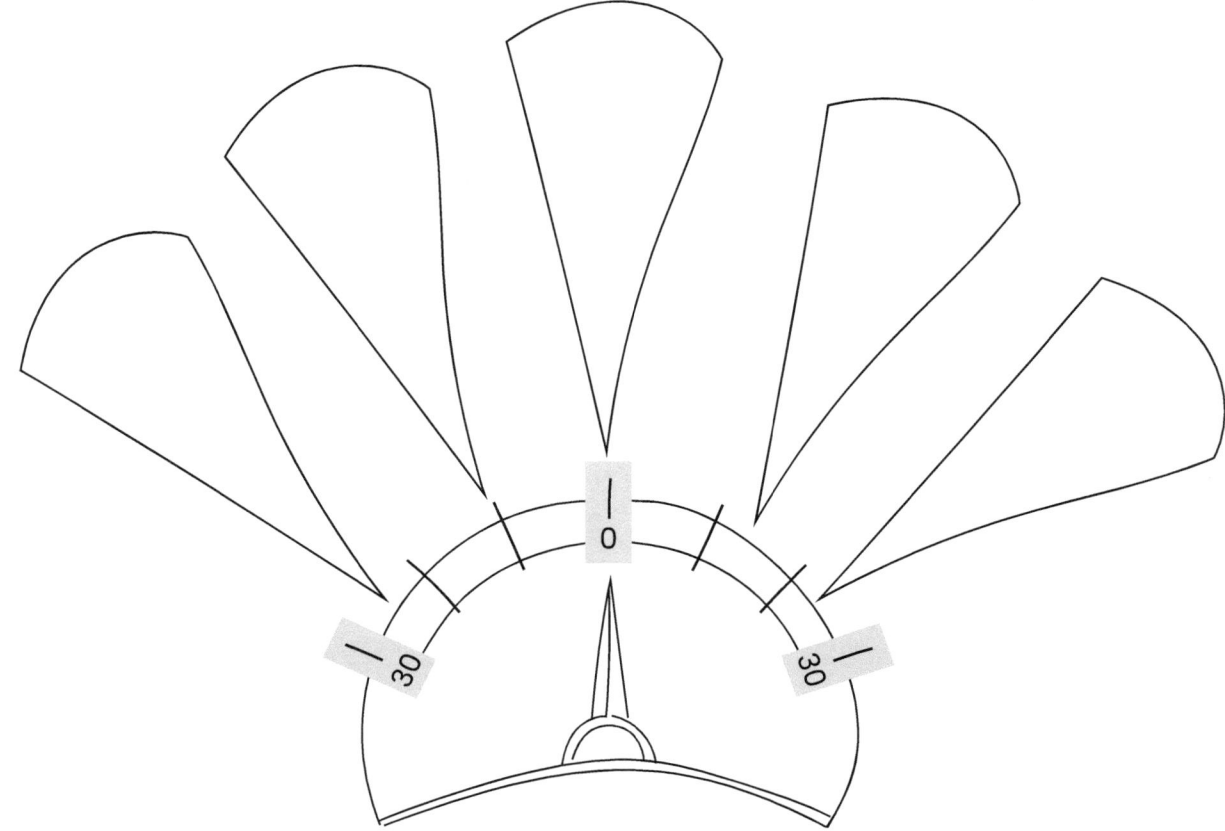

Great job.

You're halfway now.

eat
b!

Week 7

My **goals** for today

- [ ] _____
- [ ] _____
- [ ] _____

My **intentions** for the day

- [ ] _____
- [ ] _____
- [ ] _____

How did **I feel** today?

_____
_____
_____

What did **I learn**?

- [ ] _____
- [ ] _____
- [ ] _____

What went **well**?

- [ ] _____
- [ ] _____
- [ ] _____

Today, I am **grateful** for

- [ ] _____
- [ ] _____
- [ ] _____

To do tomorrow

- [ ] _____
- [ ] _____
- [ ] _____

> "The beauty of nonverbals is they're always on. They're always transmitting information for us to decode."
> – Joe Navarro

My goals for today

My intentions for the day

How did I feel today?

What did I learn?

What went well?

Today, I am **grateful** for

To do tomorrow

My **goals** for today

> "If you want to change things, you must understand how they work. Don't be afraid to ask questions about how decisions are made and how things get done."
> – Sheryl Sandberg

My **intentions** for the day

How did **I feel** today?

What did **I learn**?

What went **well**?

Today, I am **grateful** for

To do tomorrow

My **goals** for today

○ ....
○ ....
○ ....

My **intentions** for the day

○ ....
○ ....
○ ....

How did **I feel** today?

○ ....
○ ....
○ ....

What did **I learn**?

○ ....
○ ....
○ ....

What went **well**?

○ ....
○ ....
○ ....

Today, I am **grateful** for

○ ....
○ ....
○ ....

To do tomorrow

○ ....
○ ....
○ ....

My **goals** for today

- ◯ ....
- ◯ ....
- ◯ ....

> "The most important thing in communication is hearing what isn't said. The art of reading between the lines is a lifelong quest of the wise."
> – Peter Drucker

My **intentions** for the day

- ◯ ....
- ◯ ....
- ◯ ....

How did **I feel** today?

- ....
- ....
- ....

What did **I learn**?

- ◯ ....
- ◯ ....
- ◯ ....

What went **well**?

- ◯ ....
- ◯ ....
- ◯ ....

Today, I am **grateful** for

- ◯ ....
- ◯ ....
- ◯ ....

To do tomorrow

- ◯ ....
- ◯ ....
- ◯ ....

My goals for today

My intentions for the day

How did I feel today?

What did I learn?

What went well?

Today, I am **grateful** for

To do tomorrow

_____

My **goals** for today

> "Body language is a very powerful tool. We had body language before we had speech, and apparently, 80% of what you understand in a conversation is read through the body, not the words."
> – Allan Pease

My **intentions** for the day

How did **I feel** today?

What did **I learn**?

What went **well**?

Today, I am **grateful** for

To do tomorrow

_____
_____
_____
_____
_____

Reflection

What emotions did I experience most often this week, and what influenced them?

What's one positive memory from this week that I want to hold onto? Why?

What goals or priorities do I want to set for the upcoming week?

Influence Daily

Your headline:
What result did you get when you influenced others?

What symbol depicts your approach to influencing? Draw it here:

What happened when you influenced others recently? How do you know you influenced them? How did you feel?

Continue your learning: Take some time to observe someone influential at your place of work. What do they do and what could you learn from them?

Special report:
What could you try this week to be more influential?

week 8

My **goals** for today

- [ ] _____
- [ ] _____
- [ ] _____

My **intentions** for the day

- [ ] _____
- [ ] _____
- [ ] _____

How did **I feel** today?

_____
_____
_____

What did **I learn**?

- [ ] _____
- [ ] _____
- [ ] _____

What went **well**?

- [ ] _____
- [ ] _____
- [ ] _____

Today, I am **grateful** for

- [ ] _____
- [ ] _____
- [ ] _____

To do tomorrow

- [ ] _____
- [ ] _____
- [ ] _____

"The world is changed by your example, not by your opinion."
– Paulo Coelho

My goals for today

My intentions for the day

How did I feel today?

What did I learn?

What went well?

Today, I am grateful for

To do tomorrow

My **goals** for today

> "With influence comes responsibility. Is what you're lobbying for the best outcome for all? Who could argue with that?"
> – Sandra Thompson

My **intentions** for the day

How did **I feel** today?

What did **I learn**?

What went **well**?

Today, I am **grateful** for

To do tomorrow

My **goals** for today

○ ....
○ ....
○ ....

My **intentions** for the day

○ ....
○ ....
○ ....

How did **I feel** today?

○ ....
○ ....
○ ....

What did **I learn**?

○ ....
○ ....
○ ....

What went **well**?

○ ....
○ ....
○ ....

Today, I am **grateful** for

○ ....
○ ....
○ ....

To do tomorrow

○ ....
○ ....
○ ....

My **goals** for today

- ....
- ....
- ....

> "If you think you're too small to have an impact, try going to bed with a mosquito in the room."
> – Dame Anita Roddick

My **intentions** for the day

- ....
- ....
- ....

How did **I feel** today?

- ....
- ....
- ....

What did **I learn**?

- ....
- ....
- ....

What went **well**?

- ....
- ....
- ....

Today, I am **grateful** for

- ....
- ....
- ....

To do tomorrow

- ....
- ....
- ....

My goals for today

My intentions for the day

How did I feel today?

What did **I learn**?

What went **well**?

Today, I am **grateful** for

To do tomorrow

_____

My **goals** for today

"I've learned that people will forget what you said, people will forget what you did, but people will never forget how you made them feel."
- Maya Angelou

My **intentions** for the day

How did **I feel** today?

What did **I learn**?

What went **well**?

Today, I am **grateful** for

To do tomorrow

Reflection

What emotions did I experience most often this week, and what influenced them?

What's one positive memory from this week that I want to hold onto? Why?

What goals or priorities do I want to set for the upcoming week?

Give me 5!
Coaching is good for you (and them).

Try any or all of these coaching suggestions with your colleagues and see how much value you bring into the world:

Strengths Spotting: Offer praise to colleagues for their specific strengths and talents. Be specific so they feel significant.

Powerful Questioning: Ask open-ended questions to encourage self-reflection, like "What did you learn?" or "How could you approach this differently?"

Active Listening: Paraphrase what someone says to demonstrate you've heard and understood them.

Visualisation: Guide colleagues through imagining themselves successfully completing a task or goal, encouraging them to picture the details.

Gratitude: Invite colleagues to consider and document what they're grateful for, especially if they're feeling anxious.

Feel free to make some notes about these coaching suggestions at the back of this journal.

People sacrifice the **present** for the **future**. But life is available only in the present.

That is why we should walk in such a way that every step can bring us to the here and the now.

**Thich
Nhat
Hanh**

My **goals** for today

- [ ] _____
- [ ] _____
- [ ] _____

My **intentions** for the day

- [ ] _____
- [ ] _____
- [ ] _____

How did **I feel** today?

- [ ] _____
- [ ] _____
- [ ] _____

What did **I learn**?

- [ ] _____
- [ ] _____
- [ ] _____

What went **well**?

- [ ] _____
- [ ] _____
- [ ] _____

Today, I am **grateful** for

- [ ] _____
- [ ] _____
- [ ] _____

To do tomorrow

- [ ] _____
- [ ] _____
- [ ] _____

My **goals** for today

My **intentions** for the day

How did **I feel** today?

What did **I learn**?

What went **well**?

Today, I am **grateful** for

To do tomorrow

My **goals** for today

> "If you want to lift yourself up, lift up someone else."
> – Marian Wright Edelman

My **intentions** for the day

How did **I feel** today?

What did **I learn**?

What went **well**?

Today, I am **grateful** for

To do tomorrow

My **goals** for today

○ ....
○ ....
○ ....

My **intentions** for the day

○ ....
○ ....
○ ....

How did **I feel** today?

○ ....
○ ....
○ ....

What did **I learn**?

○ ....
○ ....
○ ....

What went **well**?

○ ....
○ ....
○ ....

Today, I am **grateful** for

○ ....
○ ....
○ ....

To do tomorrow

○ ....
○ ....
○ ....

My **goals** for today

- ....
- ....
- ....

> "The best coaching doesn't just teach you skills; it instills confidence, creativity, and the courage to innovate."
> — Trelise Cooper

My **intentions** for the day

- ....
- ....
- ....

How did **I feel** today?

....
....
....

What did **I learn**?

- ....
- ....
- ....

What went **well**?

- ....
- ....
- ....

Today, I am **grateful** for

- ....
- ....
- ....

To do tomorrow

- ....
- ....
- ....

My goals for today

My intentions for the day

How did I feel today?

What did I learn?

What went well?

Today, I am **grateful** for

To do tomorrow

My **goals** for today

> "The greatest gift a mentor can give is belief. When someone believes in you, it gives you the courage to take risks and pursue your dreams."
> – Holly Ransom

My **intentions** for the day

How did **I feel** today?

What did **I learn**?

What went **well**?

Today, I am **grateful** for

To do tomorrow

Reflection

What emotions did I experience most often this week, and what influenced them?

What's one positive memory from this week that I want to hold onto? Why?

What goals or priorities do I want to set for the upcoming week?

How true is it?

Such a simple question, yet it is proven to be so powerful.
How true is it? is a question you can ask yourself. It's an excellent way to challenge our assumptions or our **limiting beliefs**. To complete this exercise write down something you think isn't helpful or isn't positive. This approach helps you to **reframe** the belief and make things possible.

Here's an example

Imagine if you had an unhelpful belief that you couldn't have a dog in your life. You could ask yourself, "How true is it that I can't have a dog in my life?" Let's explore.
Could I live with a dog full time and look after them properly? No.
Could I walk a dog at the local dogs home? Yes.
Could I have dogs for the weekend from a borrow-a-dog app? Yes.
Could I have a dog overnight from the local dogs home? Yes.
Could I foster a dog for a couple of weeks? I could try.
You could ask yourself more questions, but it's clear that the statement "I can't have a dog in my life" is not true. Now it's your turn, practise here and maybe consider this in your journalling next week. How can you adopt a more positive outlook?

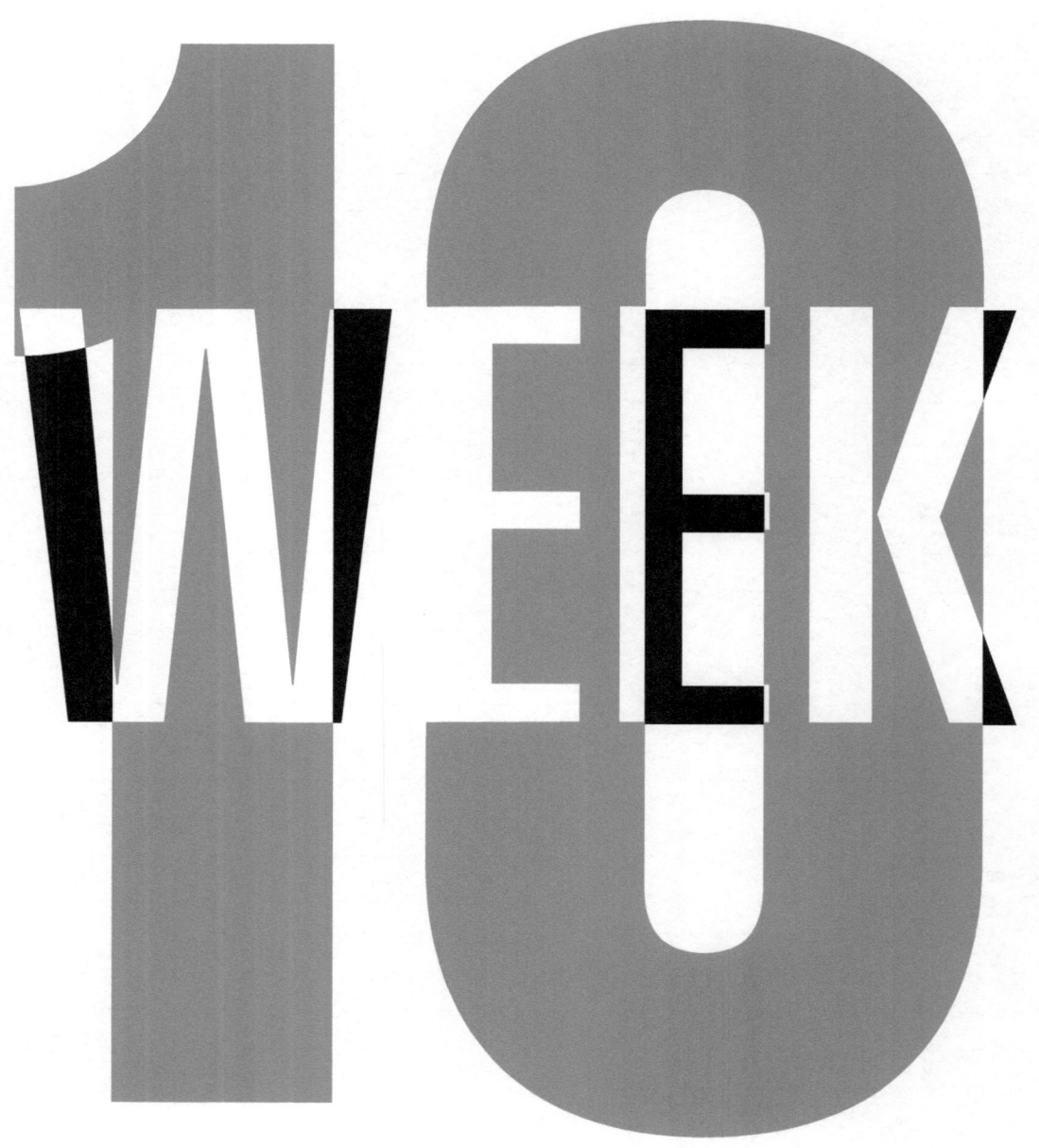

My goals for today

- [ ] _____
- [ ] _____
- [ ] _____

My intentions for the day

- [ ] _____
- [ ] _____
- [ ] _____

How did I feel today?

_____
_____
_____

What did **I learn**?

- [ ] _____
- [ ] _____
- [ ] _____

What went **well**?

- [ ] _____
- [ ] _____
- [ ] _____

Today, I am **grateful** for

- [ ] _____
- [ ] _____
- [ ] _____

To do tomorrow

- [ ] _____
- [ ] _____
- [ ] _____

My **goals** for today

My **intentions** for the day

How did **I feel** today?

What did **I learn**?

What went **well**?

Today, I am **grateful** for

To do tomorrow

My **goals** for today

> "Peace is not something you wish for; it's something you make, something you do, something you are, and something you give away. In managing conflict, it's not about winning but finding a way to move forward together."
> – Angela Merkel

My **intentions** for the day

How did **I feel** today?

What did **I learn**?

What went **well**?

Today, I am **grateful** for

To do tomorrow

My **goals** for today

○ ....
○ ....
○ ....

My **intentions** for the day

○ ....
○ ....
○ ....

How did **I feel** today?

....
....
....

What did **I learn**?

○ ....
○ ....
○ ....

What went **well**?

○ ....
○ ....
○ ....

Today, I am **grateful** for

○ ....
○ ....
○ ....

To do tomorrow

○ ....
○ ....
○ ....

My **goals** for today

- ○ ....
- ○ ....
- ○ ....

> "Never, 'for the sake of peace and quiet' deny your own experience or convictions. Conflict management requires honesty and the courage to stand by your beliefs."
> – Dag Hammarskjöld

My **intentions** for the day

- ○ ....
- ○ ....
- ○ ....

How did **I feel** today?

- ○ ....
- ○ ....
- ○ ....

What did **I learn**?

- ○ ....
- ○ ....
- ○ ....

What went **well**?

- ○ ....
- ○ ....
- ○ ....

Today, I am **grateful** for

- ○ ....
- ○ ....
- ○ ....

To do tomorrow

- ○ ....
- ○ ....
- ○ ....

My goals for today

My intentions for the day

How did I feel today?

What did I learn?

What went well?

Today, I am **grateful** for

To do tomorrow

_____

My **goals** for today

> "The salvation of this human world lies nowhere else than in the human heart, in the human power to reflect, in human humility, and in responsibility. These are the keys to managing conflict with wisdom and compassion."
> – Václav Havel

My **intentions** for the day

How did **I feel** today?

What did **I learn**?

What went **well**?

Today, I am **grateful** for

To do tomorrow

_____
_____
_____
_____
_____

Reflection

What emotions did I experience most often this week, and what influenced them?

What's one positive memory from this week that I want to hold onto? Why?

What goals or priorities do I want to set for the upcoming week?

How would you score yourself as a team player?

1 to 10

◯ **Cooperation**

◯ **Helpfulness**

◯ **Respect**

Think about yourself as a team player and write the score you would give yourself (from 1 = poor to 10 = absolutely fabulously brilliant) in the circles next to the three key characteristics of a good team player. Do others agree?

WEEK 11

My **goals** for today

- [ ] _____
- [ ] _____
- [ ] _____

My **intentions** for the day

- [ ] _____
- [ ] _____
- [ ] _____

How did **I feel** today?

_____
_____
_____

What did **I learn**?

- [ ] _____
- [ ] _____
- [ ] _____

What went **well**?

- [ ] _____
- [ ] _____
- [ ] _____

Today, I am **grateful** for

- [ ] _____
- [ ] _____
- [ ] _____

To do tomorrow

- [ ] _____
- [ ] _____
- [ ] _____

"If you want to go fast, go alone. If you want to go far, go together."
— Nelson Mandela

My goals for today

My intentions for the day

How did I feel today?

What did I learn?

What went well?

Today, I am grateful for

To do tomorrow

My **goals** for today

> "The nice thing about teamwork is that you always have others on your side."
> – Margaret Carty

My **intentions** for the day

How did **I feel** today?

What did **I learn**?

What went **well**?

Today, I am **grateful** for

To do tomorrow

My **goals** for today

○ ....
○ ....
○ ....

My **intentions** for the day   How did **I feel** today?

○ ....
○ ....
○ ....

What did **I learn**?   What went **well**?

○ ....   ○ ....
○ ....   ○ ....
○ ....   ○ ....

Today, I am **grateful** for   **To do** tomorrow

○ ....   ○ ....
○ ....   ○ ....
○ ....   ○ ....

My **goals** for today

-
-
-

> "Great teams do not hold back with one another. They are unafraid to air their dirty laundry. They admit their mistakes, their weaknesses, and their concerns without fear of reprisal."
> – Patrick Lencioni

My **intentions** for the day

-
-
-

How did **I feel** today?

-
-
-

What did **I learn**?

-
-
-

What went **well**?

-
-
-

Today, I am **grateful** for

-
-
-

To do tomorrow

-
-
-

My goals for today

My intentions for the day

How did I feel today?

What did I learn?

What went well?

Today, I am **grateful** for

To do tomorrow

My **goals** for today

> "Mountains are climbed not by one, but by many. The success of reaching the peak is shared by every team member who made it possible."
> – Tenzing Norgay

My **intentions** for the day

How did **I feel** today?

What did **I learn**?

What went **well**?

Today, I am **grateful** for

To do tomorrow

Reflection

What emotions did I experience most often this week, and what influenced them?

What's one positive memory from this week that I want to hold onto? Why?

What goals or priorities do I want to set for the upcoming week?

I HAVE A DREAM

Dr Martin Luther King Jr

Take a moment to think about a leader you are inspired by. It could be anyone.

What do they do?
How do they behave that makes you think they are inspirational?
What could you do more of to inspire others?

Feel free to write your answers at the back of this journal.

W.12.

My goals for today

- [ ] _____
- [ ] _____
- [ ] _____

My intentions for the day

- [ ] _____
- [ ] _____
- [ ] _____

How did I feel today?

_____
_____
_____

What did **I learn**?

- [ ] _____
- [ ] _____
- [ ] _____

What went **well**?

- [ ] _____
- [ ] _____
- [ ] _____

Today, I am **grateful** for

- [ ] _____
- [ ] _____
- [ ] _____

To do tomorrow

- [ ] _____
- [ ] _____
- [ ] _____

My **goals** for today

My **intentions** for the day

How did **I feel** today?

What did **I learn**?

What went **well**?

Today, I am **grateful** for

To do tomorrow

My goals for today

> "True leadership is about building others up."
> – Jacinda Ardern

My intentions for the day

How did **I feel** today?

What did **I learn**?

What went **well**?

Today, I am **grateful** for

To do tomorrow

My goals for today

○ ....
○ ....
○ ....

My intentions for the day   **How did I feel** today?

○ ....   ○ ....
○ ....   ○ ....
○ ....   ○ ....

What did **I learn**?   What went **well**?

○ ....   ○ ....
○ ....   ○ ....
○ ....   ○ ....

Today, I am **grateful** for   **To do** tomorrow

○ ....   ○ ....
○ ....   ○ ....
○ ....   ○ ....

My **goals** for today

- ....
- ....
- ....

> "True leadership is about serving others, not just leading them. It's about creating a space where everyone can thrive."
> — Jón Gnarr

My **intentions** for the day

- ....
- ....
- ....

How did **I feel** today?

- ....
- ....
- ....

What did **I learn**?

- ....
- ....
- ....

What went **well**?

- ....
- ....
- ....

Today, I am **grateful** for

- ....
- ....
- ....

To do tomorrow

- ....
- ....
- ....

My goals for today

My intentions for the day

How did I feel today?

What did I learn?

What went well?

Today, I am **grateful** for

To do tomorrow

_____

My goals for today

> "If your actions create a legacy that inspires others to dream more, learn more, do more, and become more, then, you are an excellent leader."
> - Dolly Parton

My intentions for the day

How did I feel today?

What did I learn?

What went well?

Today, I am **grateful** for

_____
_____
_____
_____
_____

Reflection

What emotions did I experience most often this week and how do these emotions compare to the patterns of emotions I described at the beginning of this 12-week journey?

Describe the most notable memory from this week. Consider the themes of all memories you have noted over the last 12 weeks.

A note from the author.

Than you

Thank you for investing in this Shine Bright™ journal and, more importantly, in yourself and your Emotional Intelligence journey.

My path with Emotional Intelligence (EQ) began 24 years ago when I discovered Dr Daniel Goleman's work, leading to my Master's dissertation on EQ in branding. In 2019, I transitioned from scholar to practitioner, becoming the UK's first Goleman Emotional Intelligence coach. The following year, I delivered my first TEDx talk, weaving together EQ, remote work, and customer experience.

The milestone year 2024 saw the launch of the Emotional Intelligence Pawdcast — where humans and their canine companions share EQ and empathy stories — and now, this journal. I'm thrilled you're embarking on your own journey with this transformative skill.

Intrigued by how EQ shapes our daily interactions and transforms customer and employee experiences?

Discover more at www.eievolution.com. There, you'll find the unique Emotional Intelligence Pawdcast and explore the diverse ways EQ can revolutionise personal and professional spheres.

Join the conversation and see how EQ is evolving the way we connect, work, and live.

Sandra

Sandra Thompson
Founding Director of Ei Evolution &
Author of Shine Bright ™ Journal

In gratitude

Marta Hereu Cuellar
Helen Eaton
Ray Cheng
Caroline Edwards
Christine Farr
Shefali Raina
Dr Daniel Goleman
Stacey Millichamp
Alexandra Galvis
Adrian Swinscoe
Dr Rod Brazier

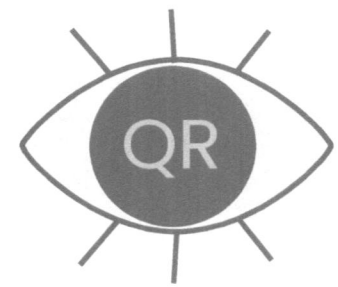

Emotional Culture Deck (page 14)		Values words (page 29)	
		Values example (page 29)	
Incredible Me (page 24)		Vision Board (page 32)	
Wow! Look how far you have come (page 26)		Energy in the room (page 116)	
The Balanced Life Tracker (page 27)		Influence daily (page 130)	

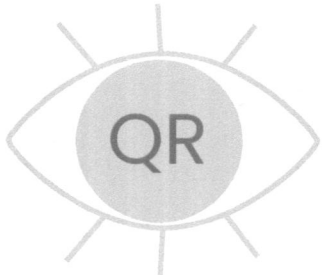

Linkedin Profile (page 195)

Ei Evolution website (page 202)

References for Shine Bright (Vol I)
Goleman, D. and Boyatzis, R.E. (2017) 'Emotional Intelligence Has 12 Elements. Which Do You Need to Work On?', Harvard Business Review, 6 February. Available at: https://hbr.org/2017/02/emotional-intelligence-has-12-elements-which-do-you-need-to-work-on (Accessed: 07.02.2019).
Goleman, D. (1995) Emotional Intelligence: Why it can matter more than IQ. Bloomsbury Publishing.
Goleman, D. (1999) Working with Emotional Intelligence. Bloomsbury Publishing.

Shine Bright ™ Volume I
First Published 2024.
Copyright © Sandra Thompson
The right of Sandra Thompson to be identified as the author of this work has been asserted in accordance with the Copyright, Designs & Patents Act 1988.
All rights reserved.
This work is protected by copyright law worldwide. While we encourage engagement with the ideas presented, we kindly ask that you respect the author's intellectual property. Any reproduction, distribution, or transmission of this publication, in whole or in part, in any form or by any means — including but not limited to photocopying, recording, scanning, retyping, or using any electronic, electrostatic, magnetic tape, digital, mechanical methods or otherwise — requires prior written consent of the copyright holder.
Brief quotations for reviews or scholarly purposes are welcome, as permitted by applicable copyright law.
This work is safeguarded under the following laws:
United Kingdom: Copyright, Designs and Patents Act 1988
United States: Copyright Act of 1976 (as amended) and related laws in Title 17 of the United States Code
European Union: Directive 2001/29/EC (Copyright Directive) and respective national implementations
China: Copyright Law of the People's Republic of China
India: Copyright Act, 1957 (as amended)
We value creativity and the sharing of knowledge. However, please note that unauthorised use, adaptation, or reproduction of this material in any manner may have legal consequences. This includes, but is not limited to, digital sharing of the content, storing of any part of this book in any type of retrieval system, online posting, or creation of derivative works without permission. We appreciate your understanding and cooperation in preserving the integrity of this work.
Published under licence by
Brown Dog Books & The Self-Publishing Partnership, 10b Greenway Farm, Bath Rd, Wick, BS30 5RL
Design by Marta Hereu Cuellar
Printed and bound in the UK
The book is printed on FSC®certified paper

ISBN 978-1-83952-857-6

Let the journey continue...

Curious about Emotional Intelligence?

Unlock a wealth of insights when you subscribe to the Ei Evolution Newsletter. Stay informed about upcoming workshops, keynote, events, short courses and new book releases.

Emotional Intelligence and empathy are vast, fascinating fields — there's always more to explore!

We're on this learning journey with you, and we'd love to hear from you. If you have some insights or suggestions for our next Shine Bright ™ journals, reach out to us at hello@eievolution.com

Let's grow our understanding of EQ and empathy, together.